West Virginia Railroads
Volume 5: Geared Logging Locomotives
Thomas W. Dixon, Jr.

Published 2012 by
TLC Publishing Inc.
18292 Forest Rd.
Forest, Virginia 24551
434-385-4076
www.tlcrailroadbooks.com

ISBN 9780939487561

Library of Congress Control Number: 2012948109

Layout and Design by
Karen Parker

Printed in the U.S.A. by
Walsworth Print Group, Marceline, Mo.

Cover Photo: Elk River No. 12 is seen here fording a stream. Note that its log flats are high class steel cars unlike many of the smaller and earlier operations which used rickety wooden cars or just separate bogey trucks without a frame. (John Krause photo, TLC Collection, black and white photo colorized by Karen Parker)

Title Page: Mower Lumber Company Shay No. 4 is heading a log train loading on the line up the mountain out of Cass in 1955. Right behind the train is a pile of logs that have been skidded out of the woods to a point of loading on the railroad. Note that the rail bed is well laid with good sawn ties and fairly good rails, not always the case on logging lines. (John Krause Photo, TLC Collection)

Opposite: Ely-Thomas Lumber Co. Shay No. 3 putters around the mill yard at Fenwick on Aug. 26, 1960. (Bob's Photos)

Back Cover Top Left: Ely-Thomas Shay No. 5 crosses Laurel Creek with a log train on its way to Jetsville in October, 1954. (August A. Thieme photo, TLC Collection)

Back Cover Top Right: Elk River Coal & Lumber Co. Shay No. 19 out in the woods loading logs on August 22, 1960. (TLC Collection)

Back Cover Middle: Elk River Coal & Lumber Co. Shay No. 19 brings a log train into Swandale, Sept. 11, 1958 (TLC Collection)

Back Cover Bottom: Meadow River Lumber Co. Shay No. 7 at the engine house in Rainelle, March 8, 1960. (TLC Collection)

Table of Contents

Introduction

The purpose of this book is to present a concise history and overview of geared locomotives used in the logging industry in West Virginia. Included are the Shay, Climax, and Heisler designs which were the three major types of geared engines.

The book is not a detailed history of the logging operations and companies which used the locomotives, nor of the construction, development, and abandonment of the lines on which they operated, but rather, it is intended to be a generalized overview for those who find the geared locomotives used in the lumbering and wood products industry of the last quarter of the 19th and first half of the 20th century of interest. Explanations of the differences of the three types of geared locomotives are presented.

An additional primary thrust of the book beyond providing basic information about the locomotives, is to show photographs of the different types on many of the logging lines in West Virginia on which they operated, demonstrating how they looked and how they were used in their normal environments.

Why West Virginia? A similar book could be written for any number of states which have a long history of logging. Certainly though, West Virginia holds a certain mystique and special interest among railfans, logging interest groups, and historians because of its rugged terrain, its relative inaccessibility though it is positioned at the center of the mid-Atlantic states, and because of the particular lure of the Appalachian cultural milieu that surrounds the state. Because its logging operations, and thus the logging railroads and their equipment, are enough different from those carried on in neighboring states, especially Pennsylvania, Virginia, and Kentucky, there is some reason to segregate it. Finally, the logging and railfan community both view West Virginia with particular interest. This interest is enhanced by the operation of the Cass Scenic Railroad State Park at Cass, West Virginia, where numerous geared locomotives take people on superb rides up the grade of the old Mower Lumber Company railroad on Spruce and Blad Knob.

The treatment of logging lines, railroads, and locomotives in West Virginia boasts a fairly extensive literature already, but most of these books are in short supply or long out of print. They include:

West Virginia Logging Railroads, William E. Warden, TLC, 1993,

Shay Logging Locomotives at Cass, W. Va. Philip V. Bagdon, TLC, 2001

Tumult on the Mountains, Roy B. Clarkson, McClain, 1964,

On Beyond Leatherbark: The Cass Saga, Roy B. Clarkson, McClain, 1990,

100 Years against the Mountain, Greenhill Station Productions, 2005,

Western Maryland Railway Shay No. 6, Greenhill Station Productions, 2010

W. Va.'s Last Logging Railroad, The Meadow River Lumber Company, Philip V. Bagdon, TLC 2002,

West Virginia's Mann's Creek Narrow Gauge Railroad, Ron Lane and Ted Schnepf, TLC, 1999,

just to name a few. There is also a fairly active historical society devoted to logging operations in West Virginia (The Mountain State Railroad and Logging Association).

The Shay Locomotive, Titan of the Timber (Michael Koch, World Press, 1971), and *Lima, The History* (Eric Hirsimaki, Hundman Publishing, 2nd Edition, 2004) are additional books that treat the Shay locomotive in some detail. The Climax has a very sparse literature and the most complete book is *Climax, An Unusual Steam Locomotive* (Thomas T. Tabor III, Railroadians of America, 1960). The Heisler is covered by *The Heisler Locomotive, 1891-1914* (B.F. Kline, Jr., B. F. Kline, Jr., 1982). The purpose, therefore, of this book is to further supplement material covered by these good books, and to add a general overview tailored directly to the engines themselves. A good source for early logging operations in West Virgina used in the preparation of this text is *The Semi-Centennial*

This medium sized saw mill at Burner, West Virginia is fairly typical of operations in the era 1910-1940. This view was taken about 1920, and we see at left a log train arriving powered by a very small Shay. At right is the lumber loading dock with three box cars positions to be loaded with lumber. For power plants mills used large boilers and engines fueled by wood refuse from the sawing process. (TLC Collection)

History of West Virginia, (James Morton Callahan, University of Michigan Press, 1913).

At first we should explain what is meant by "geared locomotive." The geared steam locomotive is a design that was first created by Ephraim Shay in 1881, especially for use on logging railroads. The contemporary Climax and Heisler designs used similar principles. Although the geared locomotive was most often used in logging operations, it was also used in other industrial switching, but on a much smaller scale. Conversely, rod locomotives were sometimes used in logging operations, where conditions permitted, but in very small numbers comparatively. The largest logging user of rod locomotives in West Virginia was the Cherry River Boom and Lumber Company, of Richwood.

Ephraim Shay simply took a short flat car and installed on it a vertical boiler with water and fuel supply. He then installed two cylinders pointed vertically. These cylinders propelled a drive shaft that ran to one of the two 4-axle trucks under the car-cum-locomotive. Through a series of gears, the mechanical power of the cylinders and shaft was then transferred to the axles. In later designs all axles were powered. Thus, all wheels of the locomotive were small-diameter driving wheels, and all weight of the locomotive, including fuel and water, was on the drivers. This helped with traction. Since each truck could swivel independently, a great degree of flexibility also was achieved, which was not possible with a rod locomotive. Indeed, logging lines often had curves of 30 degrees and more. These two elements made the geared locomotive ideal for the logging lines, which were crudely built, had very steep grades and sharp curves, were constructed without ballast and used light rails, or even wooden stringers for rails. Shay engines later developed into a more complex design with a standard horizontal boiler/firebox and locomotive cab. The only difference in appearance, and it was a major one, was that the cylinders (either two of three) were on the right side of the boiler, which was offset from center of the machine. The largest had three trucks as the fuel supply behind the cab was extended, or even four trucks as an attached "water tender" trailed the main part of the locomotive. Even this tender's weight was used for tractive power by having powered trucks under it as well, thus the four trucks.

The Climax and Heisler types used the same principle as the Shay except in the way that they transmitted the power to the wheels, as will be explained in the following chapters.

The Shay always dominated the geared type,

Typical of the large scale mill is the big plant at Cass seen here about 1940 when it was operated by the West Virginia Pulp and Paper Company. After about 1941, the mill was operated by Mower Lumber Company until its end in 1960. The Greenbrier Branch of the C&O Railway as built to accommodate this mill. Of course other mills sprang up along the line and it remained profitable as long as the timber held out. Today the ruins of this mill are visible at Cass to the many tourists who ride the Cass Scenic Railroad. (WESTVACO photo, TLC Collection)

though many Climxes were used. The Heisler type was a distant third in the business. Shays dominated in West Virginia, with a total of 170 bought new one time or another as opposed to 131 Climaxes, with very few (13) Heislers. However, photographically we have many more Shay photos than either Climaxes or Heislers. It should be noted that these figures reflect only the new locomotives ordered for use in the state. Many of the engines were sold second, third, or even fourth-hand as logging operations went out of business and new ones started up. There is no easy way to trace all this, so the numbers used are just for those known.

Logging began in what is now West Virginia (then the Trans-Alleghany section of Virginia) in the 1700s, as settlers made their way west and used the logs for homes. As hewn lumber be-

came standard for new buildings, the demand increased, and eventually water-powered saw mills using sash saws were established cutting lumber on a fairly small scale (about 500 board-feet per day for a two-man mill), though much faster than men could do by hand. By the 1840s the steam-powered circular saw came into use, which allowed an industrial-scale production of lumber for the first time. This new method arrived just as the demand for lumber increased as the area developed. A good sized circular saw mill could produce upwards of 30,000 board feet per day. The circular saw remained in use throughout the high-era of lumbering in West Virginia. The largest of these mills, the St. Lawrence Boom & Lumber Company, located at Ronceverte, could produce 120,000 board feet of lumber per day.

It was, however, the band saw that revolutionized lumbering, as the huge continuous band blades could saw lumber with a single steel band of about 2-3 feet wide and 30-45 feet long, running continuously over wheels of 5-11 feet in diameter holding the band taut. West Virginia eventually had about 250 such mills at one time or another. Some had bands with blades on both sides allowing lumber to be cut in two directions of flow at once, thus increasing output by almost 100% using the same power (more about the mills in the Chapter 1, beginning page 12).

Because of its isolated, lightly populated, mountainous land, the virgin forests of West Virginia stood longer than those in other areas where development came sooner. Lack of good transportation over the rugged territory, other than by river, inhibited growth of civilization in the region. Indeed, this resulted in the growth of a culture and civilization that was markedly different from the eastern portions of Virginia. Economic and political tensions were strong between the Trans-Alleghany region and the eastern section of the Commonwealth in the early years, and came to a crisis during the War Between the States, when the western counties seceded from Virginia after it left the Union, created the new state of West Virginia, which then joined the Union.

After the war, West Virginia's development began to increase with the coming of important railroads in both the northern region with expansion of the existing Baltimore & Ohio system, and the southern area with the building of the Chesapeake & Ohio, followed by the Norfolk & Western (and finally by the Virginian at the very late date of 1909). These railroads were concerned mainly with opening West Virginia's greatest natural resource: coal. However, they also facilitated what became the state's second most important extractive industry: lumber.

As logging developed with the circular and band mills fed by logging railroads began a large-scale production, and by 1889 302,000,000 board feet of lumber was cut in the state. This increased over the years to a high point of 1,473,000,000 board feet in 1909, and then declined to 445,000,000 by 1963. Throughout this era the logging railroad was predominant.

Just as railroads opened the state and provided access to the markets of the nation, it was railroad technology that changed and improved the way that the logging operations themselves functioned. At first the mills were located near the stands of timber that they were processing, but as the easily accessible trees were depleted,

This is a 1940s era view of sawyers operating inside a medium sized sawmill at Jennison. It gives a good impression of how the working conditions and environment were in the era. (TLC Collection)

This Lima Locomotive Works builder's portrait photo of Birch Valley Lumber Company (Tioga, Nicholas County) large three truck, 70-Ton Shay No. 5 built in December 1922. This locomotive survives today as Cass Scenic Railroad's No. 4. (TLC Collection)

the need to go farther back into the woods to acquire the logs for the mill became necessary. Delivering logs to mill was at first done with draft animals; mainly horses and mules. Later systems of troughs were developed, through which logs could side down a grade, often aided by lubricants. The principal way of moving cut logs over distance was by water on rivers. The logs were sometimes tied into rafts and men rode and guided them down a stream to the mill. All of these methods had several limitations, but these were easily overcome by railroads.

The logging railroad became the central and highly effective way to move logs from the woods to the mill. But again, it was the particular type of railroad using the peculiar geared locomotives as mentioned above, which allowed this. With grades of sometimes 10%, uneven roadways and sharp curves, as well as light rails, the geared locomotive proved its worth as the motive power for this very specialized railway application.

The loggers were further helped by the invention of the steam powered log skidder. A highly complicated machine with booms and cables, it dragged logs from the cutting area to the railroad where log loaders could hoist them onto flat cars or tied them to separate boggy-trucks for transport to the mill, where they were usually dumped into a large pond, from which they were later inserted into the mill for sawing.

This book will tell the story, mainly in photos, of the geared locomotives as they supplied logs from the woods to the mills in West Virginia's forests.

I hope that this book will give both the novice and the aficionado some interesting information and photos that will enhance further the understanding and appreciation for the varied and interesting logging operations in West Virginia.

I am particularly grateful for the many photographers, living and dead, who helped to preserve this great heritage through their fine images. We want to express a special thanks to Ken Smith of McClain Printing Co., in Parsons, W. Va., for his kind permission to use the rosters of Shays, Climaxes, and Heislers used in West Virginia first printed in Roy B. Clarkson's classic *Tumult on the Mountains* (first published in 1964, reprinted many times since, and still the in-print standard history of logging in West Virginia).

NOTE: Place names generally are not followed by the state designation, as they are all West Virginia, unless needed for clarity. The exception is if it was thought that the reader might not recognize the word as a place name, then the state ("W. Va.") is placed after it.

Thomas W. Dixon, Jr.
Lynchburg, Virginia
June 2012

This photo well illustrates the particular mechanism used by the Climax type locomotives, Shay's nearest competitor. The Climax looked a lot more like a regular rod engine with its centered boiler and two cylinders, one on each side, but there the similarity stopped. The cylinders are set at 40° angle and power a central gearbox which transmits power to the trucks via a central drive shaft. This is Elk River Coal & Cumber Company's No. 3 at Dundon May 29, 1955, fairly late in the logging railroad era. (Charles W. Winters Photo, TLC Collection)

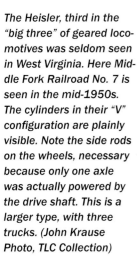

The Heisler, third in the "big three" of geared locomotives was seldom seen in West Virginia. Here Middle Fork Railroad No. 7 is seen in the mid-1950s. The cylinders in their "V" configuration are plainly visible. Note the side rods on the wheels, necessary because only one axle was actually powered by the drive shaft. This is a larger type, with three trucks. (John Krause Photo, TLC Collection)

The left side of a Shay was rather odd looking because the vertical cylinders were all positioned on the right side. Most photographers preferred the cylinder side when possible, so even though the left side shows little in the way of the Shay mechanism, photos are fairly uncommon. This engine, Ely-Thomas No. 5, is a narrow gauge version with the screen of its spark arrester raised. The spark arrester in the stack was a real necessity as these locomotives traveled in the dense woods. The long hose is for siphoning water from creeks along the line. This photo as taken at Jetsville in May 1955. (Richard J. Cook photo, TLC Collection)

This is what logging railroads helped to replace, the transportation of logs via river from woods to mill. This scene is on the Greenbrier River. (Pocahontas County Historical Society)

This close up photo taken in 1962 of Ely-Thomas Lumber Company Shay No. 2 at Fenwick shows how the vertical cylinders drove the shaft running along the right side of the trucks and through meshing gears transmitted the mechanical energy of the cylinders to the wheels. (William E. Warden photo, TLC Collection)

1: Logging in West Virginia

West Virginia was reported by observers in the late 18th and early 19th Centuries to have been covered by giant seas of trees stretching across its seeming limitless mountain ranges running from the crest of the Alleghanies, over the Appalachian plateau and down to the Ohio River in the west. This was all what is termed virgin growth, meaning it had never been cut or cleared. The only parts cut were around the small settlements of pioneers who ventured across the mountains (the "Over Mountain Men") in the early era. These great forests consisted of oak, hickory, tulip poplar, walnut, and pine. On the higher elevations were sugar maples and spruce (a 220,000 acre tract in Pocahontas County alone). Everywhere was the useful and practically indestructible chestnut tree, however it was eliminated by the blight which hit in the late 'teens, and by the early 1920s there was hardly a chestnut left alive in the entire state.

It was said that a tall man could walk through the West Virginia forests without being brushed because first limbs were often 70 or even 80 feet above ground on trees with eight or nine feet diameter. Overhead the dense foliage shut off most of the daylight and prevented underbrush growth. As late as 1870, it was estimated that more than 60 per cent of the land was still virgin forest.

To the early settlers the vast forests were at best a source of building material for their own homes and furniture, and at worst they were a nuisance that interfered with plowing and planting. When you consider that the most advanced implement

NOTE: A good deal of information about logging in West Virginia has been published in recent decades, and it has appeared in many magazines and books devoted to a number of historical subjects. In 1993 TLC Published William E. Warden's *West Virginia Logging Railroads*, which was subsequently reprinted eight times in the next 15 years. In it Warden gave a very good overview of logging in West Virginia as a prelude to his discussion of the five biggest and last logging railroads in the state. This book is now out of print, however material (slightly reworked) from his chapter on the overview of logging operations is being used now in this book as the prime source and basis for this general chapter on the same subject in this book.

a settler had for attacking a log as big in diameter as he was tall was a two-handled whipsaw, it is easy to see why timber was not considered a cash crop. Two burley men could barely turn out 100 feet of cut timber in a day with a whipsaw.

As more people moved into what is now West Virginia, the demand for cut and dressed lumber for houses, stores, banks, churches, etc., rose. This resulted in establishment of small water-powered sawmills, which began to appear just before the American Revolutionary War in the Trans-Alleghany (Alleghany will be spelled with an "a" throughout this work, since that was the preferred spelling in western Virginia) region. These mills had what amounted to a mechanized whipsaw in the form of "sash saws." These were carried on a mechanical carriage that forced the logs against the saw blades. Although a huge leap in productivity from that of sawyers with hand saws, a two-man mill could produce about 500 board feet of lumber per day. (A board foot of lumber is represented by a slab 12-inches by 12-inches and one inch thick.) This represented about a five-fold increase in the amount of lumber that could be produced over that of two men with whipsaws.

Eventually, gang saws with multiple blades were installed which could cut several boards from one log simultaneously. These more sophisticated mills could produce upwards of 30,000 board feet per day, a massive improvement over the older methods. But this was about the limit that was attained by the water powered systems.

It was the coming of the stationary steam engine powering a circular saw that wrought the greatest change in lumber production and really brought it into the industrial age.

Water mills had to be located near flowing or falling water and in times of low water the mill's output was slowed or stopped. In winter the stream often froze and halted production. But the steam powered sawmill had none of these limitations. They could be placed wherever necessary to be close to the source of the logs. They were often placed on the calm wide portions of a major

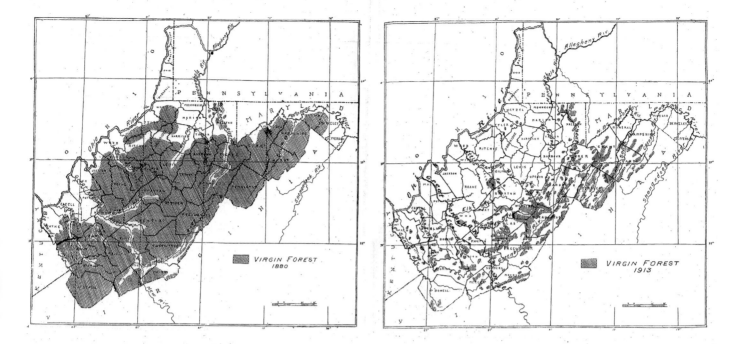

These maps show the virgin forest on West Virginia in 1880 and in 1913. It is certainly evident how effective the logging of this timber was during these 33 years. This was all made possible by the introduction of steam powered sawmills and geared locomotives operating on the logging railroads taking timber from the forest to the mills. (from Semi-Centenial History of West Virginia)

stream where logs could floated down the stream and/or held in calm water before being sawed. In areas where such a stream condition did not exist, a mill pond was usually built. Logs were then brought to the pond, placed in it for holding, and then drawn out as needed in the mill.

The steam powered mill used the circular saw which was much faster and more efficient that the sash saw. By the 1840s the steam-powered circular sawmill was established in what is now West Virginia.

However, the circular saw had some limitations. First the "kerf," which is that portion of each cut that is transformed to sawdust, needed to be limited to ½-inch or less. This restricted the diameter of circular saw because the saw blade itself had to be thicker the larger the diameter. The biggest cut, therefore, was about four feet, so many logs could not be cut into planks in a single pass through the mill. Secondly, the log could be cut in one direction only.

These limitations were overcome by the coming of yet another new technology: the band saw. First patented in France in 1834 and in the U. S. the year following, the band saw consisted on single flexible steel band ranging from 10-15 inches wide and 30-45 feet long, which ran continuously over wheels having diameters ranging from five to eleven feet. With the blade held taut by the wheels, the kerf was held at 1/4-inch regardless of the depth of the cut. Since both edges of the saw blade (band) traveled in the same direction, teeth could be cut in both edges and logs cut moving in either direction. Sawmills that used bands with teeth on both edges were known as "double-cutting band mills."

Problems with joining the two ends of the band and finding machinists who could keep the saw teeth sharp, limited the use of band mills until 1881, when the first was built at Charleston. However, band mills, because of their efficiency, became very popular. About 260 band mills were eventually operated at one time or another in West Virginia. However, they did not totally supplant the circular sawmills, which continued to operate in many areas. The largest circular sawmill ever to operate in the state was the St. Lawrence Boom and Manufacturing Company at Ronceverte, which had an output of 120,000 board feet per day.

By 1880 lumbering and coal extraction both were becoming major industries in West Virginia, and from that date until the

World War I era, it experienced great growth as the virgin forests were cut. The following figures show that growth and decline:

Year	Board Feet of Lumber
1889	302,000,000
1899	778,000,000
1909	1,473,000,000
1919	763,000,000
1929	633,000,000
1939	324,000,000
1947	484,000,000
1949	480,000,000
1963	445,000,000

As can be seen here the great growth was 1890-1910. The up-tick in production after WWII was to support the post-war housing boom.

Of course, the milling of the lumber from the logs was really the mid-point in the process of converting trees to use. The first they had to be cut down and the logs taken to the mill, then the resulting lumber had to be shipped to where it was used to construct buildings, make furniture, or be used in hundreds of other applications, so we must look at the operations in the woods.

Until the invention of the chain saw in the 1940s, the process of cutting trees varied little from that of the 19th Century. A typical logging crew consisted of six men. One was known as the "chopper" or "fitter," who was responsible for notching the tree in the direction in which it was to fall. Two "sawyers," equipped with a six-foot-long cross-cut saw would then start cutting above and on the opposite side of the notch. Wedges were then hammered into the cut they were making, to eliminate binding, and to make sure that the cut tree would fall in the direction of the notch. Once the tree was felled, the other man, called a "knot bumper" would trim off the smaller limbs and then "nose" the log, which meant cutting a bevel on each send that

This overview shows the huge mill complex at Cass, built and operated during most of its life by the West Virginia Pulp and Paper Company. The mill is at left, the lumber docks at right and in the foreground the rails of Chesapeake & Ohio's Greenbrier Branch, which was built strictly to tap the vast timber resources of eastern West Virginia. The lumber railroad joined with the C&O at a point just out of the picture to the left. This photo is from about 1951-52. (Courtesy William P. McNeel)

The West Virginia Pulp and Paper Co., had an additional mill up the mountain from Cass at Spruce which was devoted strictly to making pulp wood to be shipped down the C&O branch and over its main line to the company's giant paper mill at Covington, Va. This is a view of the large mill operation at the high and very isolated community of Spruce about 1915. (TLC Collection)

would make it easier to pull or slide the log. In addition to their regular pay, the "wood hicks" were fed at company expense four meals per day, any one of which would have been sufficient for their more sedentary kinsmen for a whole day.

Hours were long and the whole process of logging was very strenuous physical labor. The men were paid $1.50 to $1.75 per day at the turn of the 20th Century, which would amount to about $60.00 in today's buying power. This was actually very good pay for the era. But to get this the wood hick worked out in the weather winter and summer, both of which could be extreme in the West Virginia forests. At the end of the day the laborer retired to a logging camp where the accommodations were Spartan. These were a hearty breed of men.

Once the tree was felled and sawed into logs of a standard length, the logs had to be gotten to a stream or in later times to a railroad to take them to the mill. This was called "skidding."

In the early days horses and sometimes mules were used to pull the logs to skids and to drive them along the skid when gravity wasn't sufficient. The skid was simply a trough of planks arranged so as to cradle the log and allow it to slide along. Lubricants from water to grease, petroleum, or even ice, were used. From this comes the term we use today of "greasing the skids."

The teamster who managed the draft animals had a very dangerous job. If a string or "train" of logs headed downhill broke loose and got out of control the diver and the horses could easily be killed or hurt. Once the logs were entered into the skid there was less danger to the team and its master.

The term "skidding" involved all aspects of getting the log to its major transportation point, be it water or rail. Therefore the planked slide was often called a "log slide." In later days, as we shall see, a steam-powered "skidder" did much of the work.

By the 1940s caterpillar tractors replaced the horse teams in most logging operations. These

15

vehicles dragged the logs over rough logging roads that basically followed the contours on the land. However, before this time, the great innovation in skidding logs was a machine produced by the Lidgerwood Company of New York. It was a large and highly complicated machine, moved by rail to its position in the woods cutting area, which consisted of a steam pulley and contained as much as 2,600 feet of 1-7/8-inch steel cable. These cables were affixed to logs and the skidder then pulled them to the loading side, where a log loader (basically a small crane) lifted them onto the log train cars. The steam skidder was used by almost all the big logging operations in West Virginia with the exception of one of the biggest, the Cherry River Boom and Lumber Company, which used horses into the 1950s. Today, an example of a skidder is on display at the Cass Scenic Railroad at its Whitaker Station.

Once the log was gotten out of the woods to a certain point it had to be transported to the mill. If the mill was close, this was relatively easy, but as timber was cut back, the distance to the mill rapidly increased. Many loggers built tram roads that consisted of planks nailed to stringers. The planks gave the horses good footing as they pulled the wagons of logs. Some loggers started nailing wooden rails to crossties and using wagons with flanged wheels, a practice common by the 1880s. Yet this was not sufficiently efficient as the roads became longer. Also, each wagon had to have a teamster, team of horses, and brakeman.

The easiest and cheapest way to transport logs longer distances was via river. However it was labor intensive as log rafts had to be lashed together to poles at right angles using "chain dogs" consisting of two wedges joined by a chain. This made disassembling the log raft at the mill easy. In other cases the logs were spiked to the cross poles. When a group of rafts was to be sent downriver each had it have a pilot who knew the river and could guide the raft around dangerous spots such as underwater rocks, rapids, shoals, etc.

If the stream was too rapid or not wide or deep enough to accommodate rafts, log drives were used. Logs were sent downstream loose in groups with a logger riding along, jumping from log to log to clear log-jams, etc. An "ark" consisting of sleeping and eating facilities for the men on the long drive, accompanied in many cases. Logs had to be freed if they went astray or ended up on the bank or in a tangle of rocks or trees, and the whole thing took a lot of skilled manpower. But, there had to be a river of considerable size between the woods and the mill. This was not often the case. At the mill site a large boom out in the rover captured the logs and sent them to the holding area where they could be drawn into the mill for sawing.

The answer to a better way of transportation was, of course, the logging railroad, and with the coming of the geared steam locomotive this became much more feasible than before.

In the new system the logs were skidded from the woods to a point convenient to load the train. This was by draft animal or using the before mentioned Lidgerwood steam log skidder. Once to the loading point a log loader hoisted the log from the ground and placed it on the train car. This was simply a crane mounted so that it could move back and forward along the length of the train on the flat cars themselves by means of rails laid on the floors of the cars. Two types often used in West Virginia were the American and the Barnhart log loaders. Another type was mounted on a car of its own that could be positioned to load the other cars one at a time. There were a couple of types of this design but the most common simply picked up a log car and placed it in front of the loaders boom, loaded the logs, then pushed it head and placed another car from behind it in front and repeated the action.

Through the boom years of logging in West Virginia, logging companies were located in hundreds of forest sites throughout the state, retreating as the virgin forests were depleted. After WWII the motor truck loaded by cranes with caterpillar tracks began to replace the train, using roughly cut roads through the woods, the method now used.

The logging railroads were crudely built, with little or no roadway preparation, no ballast, light rails, steep grades, sharp curvature, and generally very light construction, as they were

Sawyers at work inside the Commonwealth Lumber Company mill at Glenray, near Alderson as logs await their turn a the saw. (TLC Collection)

In this photo the filer is using a filling machine with a grinding wheel to sharpen a band saw at Glenray's Commonwealth Lumber Company about 1915. (TLC Collection)

often taken up and moved as different areas of the forest were logged. These requirements gave rise to the geared locomotive. All three of the major types were used in West Virginia: Shay, Climax, and Heisler, though there were very few of the latter type, which didn't enjoy a wide popularity in the Appalachian lumbering region. A chapter follows this on each of the types, and their particular characteristics, as well as rosters of those used in West Virginia.

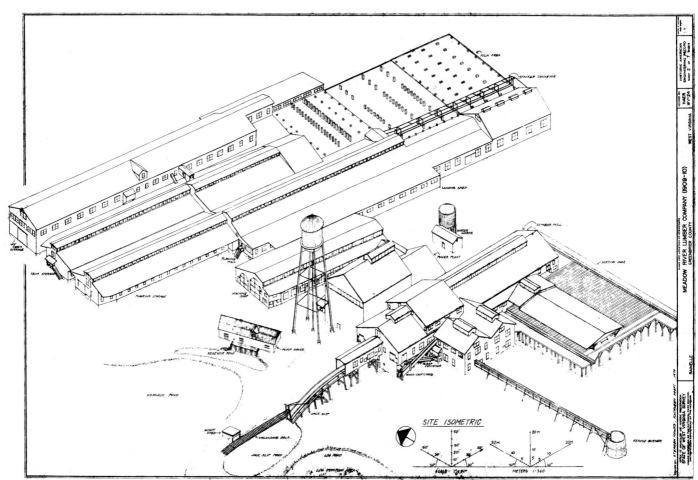

SITE ISOMETRIC

Opposite Top: One of the largest sawmills ever to operate in West Virginia was the Meadow River Lumber Company at Rainelle, seen in this aerial photo from about 1952. US Route 60 and the town are to the right. The Nicholas, Fayette & Greenbrier Railroad skirts the mill from left to right 1/3 from the top. The yard is filled with drying hardwood lumber. The mill and pond are upper center. The logging railroads built by the company were sold to the C&O and New York Central railroads and incorporated under the NF&G name. The two big railroads operated the NF&G jointly after 1932, hauling much coal in addition to the lumber from the big mill. (T. Ocheltree photo, C&O Historical Society Collection)

Opposite Below: This overview of the Meadow River Lumber Company mill at Rainelle was made before the mill was demolished. A shopping center occupies the spot today. (HABS/ HAER drawing, National Park Service)

Before the advent of logging railroads teams such as these skidded logs from the woods. They continued to be used in many operations, to get the logs to the railroad as well. (TLC Collection)

Sometimes logging railroads were built of nothing more than wooden stringers for rails. The geared locomotives could usually handle even this crude system. (TLC Collection)

August 7, 1946 and we see Mower Lumber Company Shay with a track laying gang in the woods on the mountain above Cass. Larger and more modern operations such as Mower laid down fairly heavy rail on good ties, though the roadbeds were seldom ballasted. (TLC Collection)

In this scene from the early 1950s a bit rougher line of rail is being laid down by forces of the Elk River Coal and Lumber Company up the line from Lilly Fork. (John Krause photo TLC Collection)

Three key elements are present in this scene from 1957 of the Meadow River Lumber Company's line in Greenbrier County out of Rainelle: Shay for power, Lidgerwood log skidder with its huge tower and complicated set of cables, and the log loader putting logs onto the cars. (John Krause Photo TLC Collection)

This diagram gives some appreciation for how the steam log skidder worked in dragging logs from the cutting area to the railroad. (TLC Collection)

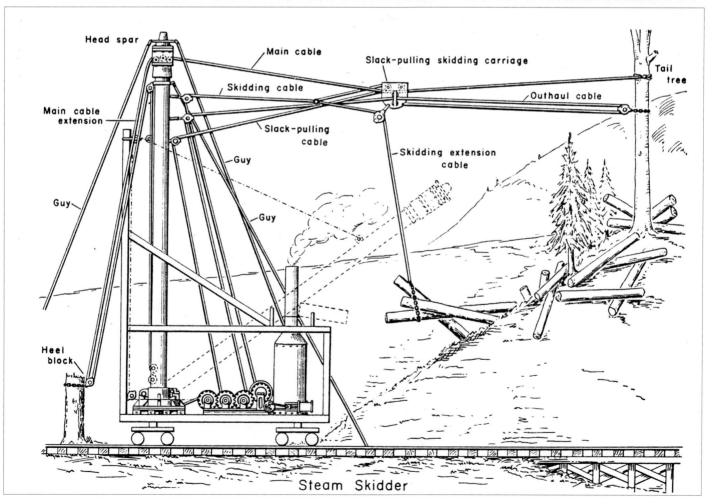

Head spar

Main cable

Slack-pulling skidding carriage

Tail tree

Skidding cable

Outhaul cable

Main cable extension

Slack-pulling cable

Skidding extension cable

Guy

Guy

Guy

Heel block

Steam Skidder

Opposite and Right: These two photos show the complicating and dangerous mechanism of the log skidder. The first shows a skidder in operation on the Mower Lumber Company line on Bald Knob near Cass and the second show a rigger working on a Mower skidder. (John Killoran and Phil Ronfor photos respectively)

W. M. Ritter Lumber Company log loader is maneuvering logs onto cars on Lilly Fork in August 1959, as Shay No. 19 idles. Once the logs were skidded to the railroad they had to be loaded by machines such as this. Note the rails laid along the cars shows the loaders can move along the train loading. (TLC Collection)

Moore Keppel & Co. American Log Loader at work in the woods. Note the small wheels on which it moved over the cars in doing this work. (TLC Collection)

Some log loaders were on their own cars. In that case they simply picked up the logging cars and moved them from one side of the loader top the other until the whole train was loaded. Obviously cars used this service were light, with just a central spine attached to trucks. (A. A. Thieme photo TLC Collection)

Shay No. 12 of the Elk River Coal and Lumber Company's line with its log loader is filling out a train from a huge pile of logs tumbled down the hillside in the early 1950s. (John Krause photo, TLC Collection)

No skidder here. Teams of horses are bringing the logs to the Cherry Boom & Lumber Company's train, powered by 2-8-2 rod locomotive No. 15. Cherry River was one of the few lumbering operations which used rod locomotives. (John Krause, TLC Collection)

Out in the woods the loggers used these makeshift and highly portable homes. This is on the Mower line up Bald Knob from Cass in August 1946. (W. Va. Collection, WVU)

Another good view of the mill from the pond side at Cass shows plenty of logs coming down the incline from the railroad and splashing into the pond. (WESTVACO photo, TLC Collection)

A jumble of elements presents itself in this May 1960 view of the Ely-Thomas mill at Fenwick. The finished lumber is stacked for drying and shipment, the log train and loader is in, a huge pile of logs is present and the mill with its characteristic stacks is in the background. (Ed Crist Photo, TLC Collection)

As mentioned in this chapter, the "other" locomotives used in logging operations were few and far between. Cherry River Boom and Lumber had a fleet of rod locomotives such as 2-8-2 No. 26 with 32 cars of logs and a box car at Donaldson May 12, 1947. (TLC Collection)

By the time diesel electric locomotives were commonly available most logging operations were closing or downsizing and when the finally gave up the geared steam locomotives they went to motor trucks. Meadow River Lumber was one that used diesels in its later era. Here No. 9 with two Meadow River cabooses pauses at the mill at Rainelle in March 1960. (William E. Warden photo, TLC Collection)

Jenningston, W.Va.

Jennings—Mill

The mill, company store, lumber yard, and large company town of Bemis in the first decade of the 20th Century crowds in the "hollow." The valleys of West Virginia were populated with many towns such as this in the high years of lumbering. (TLC Collection)

Opposite Top: This interesting view shows stacked lumber curing at the Jennings Lumber Company's mill at Jenningston, probably about 1910, with the mill and its obligatory powerhouse stacks in the background (TLC Collection)

Opposite Below: This view shows the Jenningston Mill close-up with logs being fed in and steam exhausting everywhere. (TLC Collection)

Dumping logs into the mill pond at the Meadow River Lumber Company's large plant at Rainelle, probably in the 1920s. (TLC Collection)

Although we often see lumber that is stacked at the mills as regular boards, timbers such as these being loaded into a Western Maryland gondola, as other specially cut lumber were common products of the mills. (TLC Collection)

Absent an automated skidder or other device for moving the logs from the woods, horses are being used in this view at the Cedar Grove Lumber Company. (TLC Collection)

Drying lumber stacks at the dock of the Hench, Drumgold & Shull mill at Millcreek show the tracks of the tram dollies that were used to move the boards up and down the dock. (TLC Collection)

An example of a rod locomotive in used in West Virginia logging is No. 13 of the Pardee & Curtin Lumber Company at Bergoo, seen here in about 1930. Note the shield builder's plate of the Porter Locomotive Company.

Elk River Coal and Lumber Company's No. 19 Shay is seen here next to the railbus that helped transport people up and down the company's logging railroad. At Widen May 3, 1958.(TLC Collection)

Though we often see photos of big mills, there were small ones as well. This is the part of the operation of the Rockcastle Lumber Company at Seth, with its small open structure and single spindly engine stack. This company also had a much larger industrial sized mill. The lumber in the yard seems to be mainly timbers of about the right size for use in the mines in this area. (TLC Collection)

The Boggs Stave & Lumber Company's crew is loading freshly cut logs in the ca. 1910 scene in the woods. (TLC Collection)

The Shay geared steam locomotive was the most popular of the geared style engines, and though the type saw some use as for industrial switching work, it was most often used in logging operations nationwide.

During the years of construction between 1878 and 1945 a total of 2,767 Shays were built by the Lima Locomotives Works (and its predecessor companies) in four major classes:

Class A – 2 trucks and 2 cylinders
Class B – 2 trucks and 3 cylinders
Class C – 3 trucks and 3 cylinders
Class D – 4 trucks and 3 cylinders

Of these, the most popular was the class B with 1,478 locomotives. The class A accounted for 686 and there were 542 of the class C. The class D was used mainly by class I railroads, not for logging, at least initially, and accounts for only 20 locomotives. A couple of non-standard 3 truck locomotive were built with only two cylinders for power.

Some 170 Shays were built new for West Virginia logging companies.

The genesis of the Shay was in Michigan, where Ephraim Shay conceived and patented the design. He was born in 1839, became a school teacher and then a soldier during the War Between the States. After the war he settled in Haring, Michigan, and began operating a saw mill and lumber operation. At that time one of the principal industries in the state of Michigan was lumbering.

In 1877 Shay was operating his mill and was working on a design for a specialized logging locomotive that met the needs he recognized from his recent work with logging operations employing troughs or sluices. With the help of a local machinist, Shay built his first locomotive, which had a vertical boiler connected to two vertical cylinders delivering their power via gearing to one of the two two-axle trucks, all mounted on a 14-foot flat car covered with an arched canopy roof.

The locomotive was an immediate success in Shay's logging operation. Shay and a partner took the design to the Lima Machine Works of Lima, Ohio, and the first engine was built there

This and the next three illustrations are taken from a Lima catalog, showing the four classes of Shay locomotive. (TLC Collection)

CLASS "A" SHAY LOCOMOTIVES

Boiler Pressure: 10-Ton, 150 lbs.; 13-, 18-, and 20-Ton, 160 lbs.

CODE WORD	Weight in Working Order	CYLINDERS			WHEEL BASE			DRIVERS		Capacity of Tank for Water	Fuel Capacity of Coal	Fuel Capacity of Wood	Tractive Power	HAULING CAPACITY IN TONS OF 2,000 LBS. (EXCLUSIVE ENGINE AND TENDER)							
		No.	Diam.	Stroke	Rigid	Total		No.	Diam.					On Level	ON GRADES						
															½%	1%	2%	3%	4%	5%	6%
	Tons		In.	In.	In.	Ft.	In.		In.	Gals.	Tons	Cords									
AB	10	2	5	8	36	15	4	8	20	300	¼	¼	3460	422	182	113	62	40	29	22	17
ABE	13	2	6	10	48	18	10	8	22	400	¼	¼	6050	643	326	203	113	76	55	43	34
ABLE	18	2	7	12	50	21	0	8	26	730	1	¼	8330	1023	445	280	155	104	76	58	47
ABLER	20	2	8	12	50	23	2	8	26	830	1	¼	10270	1265	551	347	194	131	96	75	60

NOTE.—Haulages on grades of 7% and up will be furnished on application.

in late 1878. The Lima company had a line of saw mill equipment as well as agricultural implements, so the locomotive fit into its line of work well. Subsequent locomotives were to have all trucks powered, important in making the design effective to its maximum capability. In 1881 Shay was issued a patent for his design and he licensed the design to Lima for continued production. He also sold certain rights to another machine works in Michigan which produced an engine of similar but somewhat different design, but only a few locomotives were built.

Lima refined the design further and sold locomotives to a variety of buyers. In the following decades the design was further enlarged and refined and the Shay geared locomotive became a standard for the logging industry. It also served to make the Lima Locomotive Works into a major locomotive builder that eventually, by the early 1900s it went into building larger rod locomotives for Class I railroads, which soon exceeded the Shays on its erecting floor as the need for new geared locomotives declined. Ultimately, in the 1920s, Lima developed the "Super Power" steam locomotive concept which resulted in the building of the largest and most powerful of all steam locomotives, used all across America. As Lima was increasing its production of rod locomotives, its production of Shays steadily declined since the logging industry peaked and was in decline by the 1920s. Also, the Shays were very often resold and resold, so the need for new engines also decreased. A company going out of business because of exhausted timber would sell its locomotives to another just starting at another location, so the need for new engines was lessened by the large after-market trade in used ones.

The Shays were durable and desirable machines that did a job so well that they became virtually the byword for the geared design, even though the Climax and Heisler types came into strong competition for the loggers' business. Today most of the geared locomotives left on display or in operation on tourist lines are Shays.

A few class I railroads tried the Shay design for some of their most difficult lines, including Southern, Western Maryland, Norfolk and

CLASS "B" SHAY LOCOMOTIVES

Boiler Pressure: 24- to 32-Ton Locomotives inclusive, 160 lbs.; 36- to 50-Ton inclusive, 180 lbs.; 60-Ton, 200 lbs.

Code Word	Weight in Working Order	Cylinders			Wheel Base			Drivers		Capacity of Tank for Water	Fuel Capacity of Coal	Fuel Capacity of Wood	Tractive Power	Hauling Capacity in Tons of 2,000 Lbs. (Exclusive Engine and Tender)							
		No.	Diam.	Stroke	Rigid	Total		No.	Diam.					On Level	On Grades						
															½%	1%	2%	3%	4%	5%	6%
	Tons		In.	In.	In.	Ft.	In.		In.	Gals.	Tons	Cords									
Bay	24	3	8	8	50	21	11	8	27½	830	1¼	1	10280	1261	548	343	190	127	93	71	56
Bale	28	3	8	10	50	24	4	8	27½	850	1½	1¼	12860	1580	687	431	240	161	118	91	72
Baler	32	3	8	12	50	25	5	8	29	1000	1¾	1½	14150	1736	754	473	263	176	129	99	78
Ballad	36	3	10	10	50	26	5	8	29	1200	1¾	1½	14320	1756	760	476	262	174	126	96	76
Balloon	42	3	10	12	50	28	6	8	29½	1560	2	1½	16900	2070	898	562	310	206	150	114	90
Baluster	50	3	11	12	52	28	10	8	32	1750	3¼	2	22580	2775	1205	767	421	282	206	159	126
Balustrad	60	3	12	12	56	32	8	8	36	2000	3¾	2	23890	2928	1267	793	438	291	211	161	126

Note.—Haulages on grades of 7% and up will be furnished on application.

Western and Chesapeake & Ohio. The C&O was the biggest Class I railroad user of Shays with 16 on its roster, all used in West Virginia on steep branches reaching coal mines in the New River coal fields. Later some of these giant engines were sold to logging operators.

The pioneering aspect of Shay's design first was that it allowed relatively small driving wheels (usually 36-inches or so in diameter) to support the entire locomotive weight. Since the water and fuel supplies were carried on the main engine, all of their weight was also carried on the drivers, thus giving them even better traction. Also, since all the wheels were powered equally on both sides since the power from the cylinder was transmitted to the axles through the gears, they provided a much more even torque. Regular rod locomotives' cylinders were applying power to each set of drivers at alternative intervals, side to side, and stroke-by-stroke, thus causing dynamic augment or "pounding" on rails and uneven torque side-to-side. Also, each of the Shay trucks was free to swivel and "hunt" from side to side as needed, with a very short wheel-base. This in ef-

fect made the Shays part of the "articulated" style of locomotives in that separate sets of drivers could move separately under the same boiler, yet markedly different from the huge rod-connected articulated locomotives. This articulation applied as well to Climaxes and Heislers, of course.

Another important part of the design was that since the drivers were small and mounted in trucks (essentially just freight car wheels mounted on an enlarged freight car style truck. The trucks had a very short rigid wheel base and could swivel freely since they were mounted to the locomotive frame only with a king-pin in the same way that freight car truck was mounted to its frame. This all allowed the Shay to have a great flexibility as it traveled over uneven track, around sharp curves, and over light rail, all characteristics that set it apart from the standard rod engine.

Because all the weight of the entire locomotive was on the driving wheels, added to the fact that they were so small and that they were connected to the cylinder with gears, helped to make the engine a virtual mountain climber, able to go up

CLASS "C" SHAY LOCOMOTIVES
Boiler Pressure, 200 lbs.

CODE WORD	Weight in Working Order	CYLINDERS			WHEEL BASE			DRIVERS		Capacity of Tank for Water	Fuel Capacity of Coal	Fuel Capacity of Wood	Tractive Power	HAULING CAPACITY IN TONS OF 2,000 LBS. (EXCLUSIVE ENGINE AND TENDER)							
		No.	Diam.	Stroke	Rigid	Total		No.	Diam.					On Level	ON GRADES						
						Ft.	In.								½%	1%	2%	3%	4%	5%	6%
	Tons		In.	In.	In.	Ft.	In.		In.	Gals.	Tons	Cords									
CAP	70	3	12	15	52	40	2	12	36	3000	5	2	30350	3723	1616	1014	562	376	275	211	167
CARE	80	3	13½	15	56	44	6	12	36	3000	5	....	35100	4305	1868	1169	648	434	317	242	192
CARAT	90	3	14½	15	56	43	3½	12	36	3500	5	....	40400	4960	2156	1353	752	504	369	284	225
CARBON	100	3	15	17	58	45	6	12	40	4000	6	....	44100	5411	2349	1470	819	548	400	308	244
CAPTURE	125	3	17	18	64	46	10	12	46	4000	9	....	53000	6500	2817	1768	979	654	477	366	289

NOTE.— Haulages on grades of 7% and up will be furnished on application.

much steeper grades than an road engine, which would tend to slip and stall. Shays could negotiate grades of up to 10-to-13 percent with a load, whereas a rod engine could hardly make it up a third of this grade itself, let along handling a load.

With all these peculiar and special features, the Shay allowed the logging company, with its rough, uneven, curvy, steep, temporary, un-ballasted track, to get its railroad back into the woods and extract the timber by the train-load to the sawmill. Since before the coming of the geared engine design the cost of lumber was over 70% consumed with transportation, this number was markedly improved, allowed for better profit for the sawmill operator, and better pricing for its product. This all added to the growth of the lumbering industry in the latter quarter of the 19th Century.

The Shay really put the Lima Locomotive Works on the map of locomotive builders, but as mentioned above it soon went into the production of rod engines and this part of its business soon took over the production to the extent that the Shay production was very much a sideline, while the major rod engine types made a bid to challenge the other big steam locomotive builders of the country including Baldwin and American (which didn't build geared engines at all). With the introduction of the 2-8-4 type and its "Super Power" concept in the mid-1920s Lima really reshaped the whole steam locomotive design right up to the end of steam.

Throughout the 1930s only seven Shays were built, and the last Shay that Lima built was a monstrous 150-ton 3-truck engine for the Western Maryland Railway in 1945 for service on its steep Chaffee coal branch (see page _____).

Although the first geared design and the most popular, the Shay's competitors, the Climax and Heisler, both had some design features that recommended them, including a central drive shaft rather than an offset one for both, and an enclosed, greased gear box in the case of the Heisler. However none had the market share or wide positive reputation of the Shay.

CLASS "D" SHAY LOCOMOTIVES
Boiler Pressure, 200 lbs.

Code Word	Weight in Working Order	Cylinders			Wheel Base			Drivers		Capacity of Tank for Water	Fuel Capacity of Coal	Tractive Power	Hauling Capacity in Tons of 2,000 Lbs. (Exclusive Engine and Tender)							
		No.	Diam.	Stroke	Rigid	Total		No.	Diam.				On Level	On Grades						
														½%	1%	2%	3%	4%	5%	6%
Dan	Tons 150	3	In 17	In. 18	In. 64	Ft. 58	In. 4	16	In. 46	Gals. 8000	Tons 9	53000	6475	2792	1743	954	629	452	341	264

Note.—Haulages on grades of 7% and up will be furnished on application.

Lima locomotive works photos showing the re-building of a three-truck Shay at Lima. From these photos one can get a better idea as to the design and makeup of the Shay engine. This engine is being rebuilt for some reason:

Triple vertical cylinder set.

New and old wooden cabs

Boiler from left side

Reassembled locomotive, awaiting final touches

Views of the power trucks under a Shay show us the gearing and how each axle was connected to the drive shaft and received its power directly by means of the meshing gears. (Lima Catalog, TLC Collection)

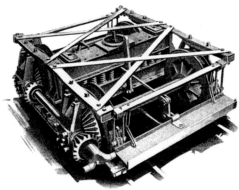

Drawing of a heavy probably 70-ton 3-truck Shay with diamond stack and water tender. By use of the third truck, under the tender, all the engine and its fuel and water were used to add to tractive effort. However, as water was used the weight on the rear truck lessened somewhat. (TLC Collection)

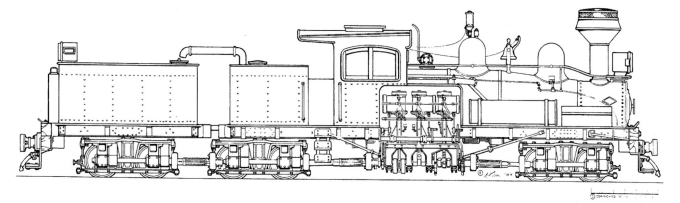

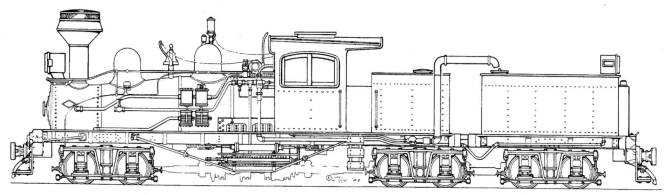

F. C. Cook Shay No. 16 at Alexander, W. Va., from the head end looks like any characteristic Shay with the offset boiler. The engineer had the advantage of being able to see all the working mechanism of the locomotive from his side. For those seeing a Shay for the first time, however, their idea of a steam locomotive was severely jarred. (TLC Collection)

Mower Lumber Company Shay No. 1 at the coaling dock, Cass, W. Va., on May 30, 1958. This locomotive is an example of how the Shay, and other geared locomotives, changed owners over time as lumber resources shifted. It began as G. W. Huntley Lumber Co. of Neola; sold to Stoner Lumber Co, at Thornwood; sold to North Fork Lumber Co, at Nottingham; sold to Greenbrier Cheat and Elk RR, Cass; transferred with the company to Mower Lumber Company. It subsequently operated on the Cass Scenic Railroad, and is now on display at the B&O Railroad Museum in Baltimore, Md., having been traded to them in exchange for the massive WM No. 6, the largest Shay built by Lima. (TLC Collection)

Owner / Location	Builder / Original owner	Year	No.
W. Va. Spruce Lbr. Co., Cass, W. Va.	8 W. Va. Spruce Lbr. Co., Cass, W. Va.	1912	2583
W. Va. Spruce Lbr. Co., Cass, W. Va.	10 ———	1914	2765
W. Va. Spruce Lbr. Co., Cass, W. Va.	11 ———	1914	2799
W. Va. Spruce Lbr. Co., Cass, W. Va.	4 (2) Tioga Lumber Co., Tioga, W. Va.	1922	3189
Grove City Lbr. Co., Greenbrier, W. Va.	Kiar(?), Kirby & Liny(?) Lbr. Co., Hinton, W. Va.	1908	2069
Groves Creek Lbr. Co., Ira, W. Va.	Bessemer Limestone, Covert, Pa.	1903	813
T. L. Hackney, Glady, W. Va.	T. L. Hackney, Glady, W. Va.	1885	131
W. A. Harris Lbr. Co., Williamson, W. Va.	H. Kalback & Son, Pickens, W. Va.	1894	467
Highland Lumber Co., Seth, W. Va. (also owned by Lackawana Coal & Lbr. Co., Charleston, W. Va.)	Lackawana Coal & Coke Co., Seth, W. Va.	1914	2701
Horsecreek Lumber Co., Julian, W. Va.	Dixie Lumber Co., St. Albans, W. Va.	1907	2028
Howard Lumber Co., Cowen, W. Va.	Smoot Lumber Co., Cowen, W. Va.	1916	2884?
Howard Lumber Co., Cowen, W. Va.	Smoot Lumber Co., Cowen, W. Va.	1910	2342
Hutchinson Lumber Co. ?, Sevy Bridge, W. Va.	Drummond & S. W. Tallapoosa Lumber Co., Sistrunk, Ala.	1894	475
Hutchinson Lumber Co. ?, Sevy Bridge, W. Va.	Drummond & S. W. Tallapoosa Lumber Co., Sistrunk, Ala.	1894	476
Hutchinson Lbr. Co., Meadow Bridge, W. Va.	Hutchinson Lbr. Co., Huntington, W. Va.	1910	2375
Hutchinson Lumber Co., Sevy Bridge, W. Va. (also owned by Seaman Lbr. Co., Huntington, W. Va.)	Hutchinson Lumber Co., Sevy Bridge, W. Va.	1913	2702
Hutchinson Lumber Co., Meadow Bridge, W. Va. (also owned by Hammill Lbr. Co., Meadow Bridge, W. Va.; by Ruthbell Lbr. Co., Elkins, W. Va.)	207 Hutchinson Lbr. Co.	1916	2871
Kendall Lbr. Co., Albright, W. Va.	Goodyear Lbr. Co., Austin, Pa.	1892	377
Kendall Lbr. Co., Albright, W. Va. (Caflish Lbr. Co.)	Caflish Lbr. Co., Albright, W. Va.	1920	3114
Kendall Lbr. Co., Albright, W. Va. (Caflish Lbr. Co.)	———	1908	1727(?)
Kendall Lbr. Co., Albright, W. Va. (Caflish Lbr. Co.)	Flint, Ewing & Stoner, Dunlevie, W. Va.	1906	1751
Kendall Lbr. Co., Albright, W. Va. (also owned by Lewis Lbr. Co., Albright, W. Va.)	Kingwood Lbr. Co., Caddell, W. Va.	1907	1955
Kendall Lbr. Co., Albright, W. Va. (also owned by Ruthbell Lbr. Co., Elkins, W. Va.)	R. Chaffey, Williams, W. Va.	1910	2312
Kendall Lbr. Co., Albright, W. Va.	Wildell Lbr. Co., Wildell, W. Va.	1905	1595
Keystone Manufacture Co., Elkins, W. Va. (Flint)	W. H. Green, Coalton, W. Va.	1910	2355
Keystone Manufacture Co., Elkins, W. Va. (Erwin)	G. G. Sitzinger, Harry Siding, W. Va.	1906	1824
Keystone Manufacture Co., Elkins, W. Va. (Erwin)	Glade Lumber Co.	1920	3067
Kingwood Lumber Co., Caddell or Kingwood, W. Va.	B. F. Hazelton, Bradford, Pa.	1892	395
Maryland Lumber Co., Denmar, W. Va. (also owned by Raine Lbr. Co., Honeydew, W. Va.)	J. A. Dennison, Beard, W. Va.	1910	2336
Moon Lumber Co., Curtis, W. Va.	Holbrook, Cabot & Rolling, Boston, Mass.	1909	2214
Morgan Lumber Co., Powellton, W. Va.	5 T. C. McVey Lbr. & Tie Co., Sanderson, W. Va.	1913	2699
Morribell Lumber Co., Morribell, W. Va.	Morrison & Bell, Morribell, W. Va.	1905	1558
Mountain Lick Lumber Co., Olive, W. Va.	P. L. & W. F. Brown, Durbin, W. Va.	1905	1602
Mountain Lick Lumber Co., Olive, W. Va.	H. J. Wilmoth, Boyer Siding, W. Va.	1910	2340
Natwick-Nixon Co., Athens, W. Va.	England-Walton & Co., Stokesville, Va.	1906	1779
A. D. Neill & Son, Clover Lick, W. Va.	F. S. Wise, Bartow, W. Va.	1910	2346
A. D. Neill & Son, Clover Lick, W. Va.	Gillfillan, Neil & Co., Neil, W. Va.	1907	1845
Newell Brothers Lbr. Co., Braucher, W. Va.	Dyer and White, Park City, Utah	1885	130
Newell Brothers Lbr. Co., Braucher, W. Va.	B. L. Rodgers, Warren, Pa.	1890	298
Northeast Lumber Co., Huntington, W. Va.	Northeast Lumber Co., Huntington, W. Va.	1924	3267
North Fork Lumber Co., Nottingham, W. Va.	W. Va. Spruce Lbr. Co., Cass, W. Va.	1900	630
North Fork Lumber Co., Nottingham, W. Va. (also owned by Wilmoth & McCullough Lbr. Co., Boyer, W. Va.)	M. P. Bock Lumber Co., Arborvale, W. Va.	1901	662
Nuzam Lumber Co., Holly, W. Va.	Bessemer Limestone Co., Covertt, Pa.	1903	813
Oak Run Lumber Co., Palmer, W. Va.	Heckmer & White, Gillespie, W. Va.	1901	665
Oakwood Lumber Co., Pickens, W. Va.	Holley Lumber Co., Parkersburg, W. Va.	1908	658
Otter Creek Boom & Lbr. Co., Davis, Hutting and Hambleton, W. Va.	2 Otter Creek Boom & Lbr. Co., Davis, Hutting and Hambleton, W. Va.	1897	532
Otter Creek Boom & Lbr. Co., Davis, Hutting and Hambleton, W. Va.	3 Otter Creek Boom & Lbr. Co., Davis, Hutting and Hambleton, W. Va.	1897	535
Otter Creek Boom & Lbr. Co., Davis, Hutting and Hambleton, W. Va.	5 Otter Creek Boom & Lbr. Co., Davis, Hutting and Hambleton, W. Va.	1904	858
Otter Creek Boom & Lbr. Co., Davis, Hutting and Hambleton, W. Va.	6 Otter Creek Boom & Lbr. Co., Davis, Hutting and Hambleton, W. Va.	1907	1947
Pardee & Curtin Lumber Co., Curtin, W. Va.	1 Pardee & Curtin Lumber Co., Curtin, W. Va.	1900	607
Pardee & Curtin Lumber Co., Curtin, W. Va.	2 Pardee & Curtin Lumber Co., Curtin, W. Va.	1901	680
Pardee & Curtin Lumber Co., Curtin, W. Va.	3 Pardee & Curtin Lumber Co., Curtin, W. Va.	1904	913
Pardee & Curtin Lumber Co., Curtin, W. Va.	4 Pardee & Curtin Lumber Co., Curtin, W. Va.	1905	1524
Pardee & Curtin Lumber Co., Curtin, W. Va.	5 Pardee & Curtin Lumber Co., Curtin, W. Va.	1905	1591
Pardee & Curtin Lumber Co., Curtin, W. Va.	7 Pardee & Curtin Lumber Co., Curtin, W. Va.	1907	2018
Pardee & Curtin Lumber Co., Curtin, W. Va.	9 Pardee & Curtin Lumber Co., Curtin, W. Va.	1910	2311
Pardee & Curtin Lumber Co., Curtin, W. Va.	10 Pardee & Curtin Lumber Co., Curtin, W. Va.	1911	2405
Parkersburg Tie and Lbr. Co., Parkersburg, W. Va.	1 Parkersburg Tie and Lbr. Co., Parkersburg, W. Va.	1907	1805
Parsons Pulp & Lumber Co., Horton, W. Va.	Buckhannon River Lbr. Co.	1893	443
Parsons Pulp & Lumber Co., Horton, W. Va. (also owned by J. L. Rumbarger Lbr. Co., Dobbins, W. Va.)	5 J. L. Rumbarger, Dobbins, W. Va.	1896	500
Parsons Pulp & Lumber Co., Horton, W. Va. (also owned by J. L. Rumbarger Lbr. Co., Dobbins, W. Va.)	3 J. L. Rumbarger, Dobbins, W. Va.	1901	660
Parsons Pulp & Lumber Co., Horton, W. Va.	7 W. S. Tolbard	1902	742
Parsons Pulp & Lumber Co., Horton, W. Va.	Condon Lane Boom & Lbr. Co., Whitmer, W. Va.	1904	853
Parsons Pulp & Lumber Co., Horton, W. Va.	4 Dry Fork Lumber Co., Laneville, W. Va.	1905	970
Parsons Pulp & Lumber Co., Horton, W. Va.	Parsons Pulp & Lumber Co., Horton, W. Va.	1910	2223
Parsons Pulp & Lumber Co., Horton, W. Va.	Parsons Pulp & Lumber Co., Horton, W. Va.	1911	2455

Owner / Location	Builder / Other Owner	Year	No.
Parsons Pulp & Lumber Co. Horton, W. Va. (also owned by Whitmer Parsons Pulp & Paper Co., Horton, W. Va.)	10 Parsons Pulp & Lumber Co. Horton, W. Va.	1913	2674
Pocahontas Lumber Co. Burner, W. Va.	E. R. Monroe Crystal Hill, Va.	1904	927
Pocahontas Lumber Co. Burner, W. Va.	2 Pocahontas Lumber Co. Burner, W. Va.	1904	929
Pocahontas Lumber Co. Burner, W. Va.	3 Pocahontas Lumber Co. Burner, W. Va.	1906	1603
Raine-Andrews Lumber Co. Gladwin or Evenwood, W. Va.	Jas. B. Reed Co. Slate Run, Pa.	1904	919
Raine-Andrews Lumber Co. Gladwin or Evenwood, W. Va.	2 Raine-Andrews Lumber Co. Evenwood, W. Va.	1902	740
Raine-Andrews Lumber Co. Gladwin or Evenwood, W. Va.	3 Raine-Andrews Lumber Co. Evenwood, W. Va.	1904	924
Raleigh Lumber Co. Raleigh, W. Va.	Cobbs & Mitchell, Inc. Cadillac, Mich.	1904	889
Raleigh Lumber Co. Raleigh, W. Va.	Marion & Rye Valley Marion, Va.	1904	960
Raleigh Lumber Co. Raleigh, W. Va.	Fosburg Lumber Co. Portsmouth, Va.	1905	980
Raleigh Lumber Co. Raleigh, W. Va. (also owned by Wm. Ritter Lbr. Co., Maben, W. Va.)	Stearns Lumber Co. Stearns, Ky.	1905	1530
Raleigh Lbr. Co. Raleigh, W. Va.	Readen Copper Co.	1914	2801
Wm. Ritter Lumber Co. Maben, W. Va. (also owned by J. L. Rumbarger Lbr. Co., Dobbins, W. Va.)	Mancelona Handle Co. Mancelona, Mich.	1896	501
Wm. Ritter Lumber Co. Maben, W. Va.	Kettle Creek Coal Co. Bitumen, Pa.	1899	581
Wm. Ritter Lumber Co. Maben, W. Va.	Mitchell Bros. Cadillac, Mich.	1903	778
Wm. Ritter Lumber Co. Maben, W. Va.	1 Wm. Ritter Lumber Co. Mortimer, N. C.	1905	987
Wm. Ritter Lumber Co. Maben, W. Va.	Shenango Furnace Co. Hibbing, Minn.	1907	1862
Wm. Ritter Lumber Co. Maben, W. Va.	W. M. Carney Mill Co. ?	1916	2804
Robinson Lumber Co. Richwood, W. Va.	Hollywood Lumber & Coal Hollywood, W. Va.	1910	2286
S. D. Shevrick Lumber Co. Hendricks, W. Va.	Cutler & Savinge Lbr. Co. Roaring Creek Jct., W. Va.	1882	50
Sliger Brothers Jerguson, W. Va.	Paramie? Coal & Mining Co.?	1909	2189
R. C. Stave & Lumber Co. Brownsville, W. Va.	John Raine & Co. Millpoint or Seebert, W. Va.	1907	1991
L. O. Steinbeck Lbr. Co. Plymouth, W. Va. (also owned by Waggy & Harder Lbr. Co., Sutton, W. Va.)	Waggy & Harder Lumber Co. Sutton, W. Va.	1909	2224
Steinbeck & Osborne Blakely?, W. Va.	Steinbeck & Osborne Blakely?, W. Va.	1910	2188
Steinbeck & Osborne Blakely?, W. Va.	Steinbeck & Osborne Blakely?, W. Va.	1909	2211
The Sun Lumber Co. Weston, W. Va.	Henry Spies Pickens, W. Va.	1904	894
Thompson Lumber Co. Davis, W. Va.	Miller & Whitmer Bugaro, W. Va.	1889	237
Tolbert Lumber Co. Beckley, W. Va.	R. L. Brown Lumber Co.?	1901	654
E. Vansickle Co. Trowbridge, W. Va.	Brown Lumber Co. Belington, W. Va.	1909	2209
Whitmer Parsons Pulp & Paper Co. Horton, W. Va.	8 Whitmer Parsons Pulp & Paper Co. Horton, W. Va.	1907	1995
Waggy & Harder Lumber Co. Sutton, W. Va.	Henry Waggy Lbr. Co. Sutton, W. Va.	1905	1581
J. S. Walker Lumber Co. Okeefe, W. Va.	W. G. Ward Ironton, Ohio	1900	616
Warne Lumber Corp. Raywood, W. Va.	Cranberry R. R. Seebert, W. Va.	1905	997
Warne Lumber Corp. Raywood, W. Va.	Cranberry R. R. Seebert, W. Va.	1906	1784
West Virginia Timber Co. Charleston, W. Va.	West Virginia Timber Co. Charleston, W. Va.	1908	2068 ?
Wilderness Lumber Co. Charleston, W. Va. (Nallen, W. Va.)	Interstate Cooperage Co. Gassaway, W. Va.	1910	2343
Wilderness Lumber Co. Charleston, W. Va. (Nallen, W. Va.)	Clay Lumber Co. Middlefork, W. Va.	1914	2807
Wilderness Lumber Co. Charleston, W. Va. (Nallen, W. Va.)	2 Wilderness Lumber Co. Charleston, W. Va.	1917	2892
Wilderness Lumber Cc. Charleston, W. Va. (Nallen, W. Va.)	3 Wilderness Lumber Co. Charleston, W. Va.	1917	2953
Wilderness Lumber Co. Charleston, W. Va. (Nallen, W. Va.)	5 Wilderness Lumber Co. Charleston, W. Va.	1926	3303
Yomack Lbr. Co. Buckhannon, W. Va.	Beaver Creek Lumber Co. Davis, W. Va.	1896	508

This roster is taken from *Tumult on the Mountain* by Roy B. Clarckson and used with permission of McClain Printing Co., Parsons, W.Va.

This somewhat fuzzy photo shows Greenbrier, Cheat & Elk 150 ton four truck Shay No. 13 at Cass. This engine was bought from the C&O and was used to haul log trains over the mountain from Spruce to Cass. (Karen Parker Collection)

The second most popular geared locomotive was the Climax type, manufactured by the Climax Manufacturing Company of Corry, Pennsylvania. This design had a number of variants.

Records/documentation on the Climaxes are sketchy, but it appears that about 1,060 locomotives were built. Of these 131 were bought new by logging companies in West Virginia, a number just 39 fewer than Shays.

As with the Shay, the Climax came is several models:

Class A - This type, built throughout the period of Climax construction had a horizontal boiler, with cylinders that were located in the cab and transferred power to a drive shaft under the center of the locomotive. It was built on a flat car type frame arrangement, and had a canopy that covered the whole thing except for the front of the boiler and smoke box. It did not have the appearance of a conventional steam locomotive at all, and was built in sizes up to 22 tons. The earlier models of this class had a vertical boiler and firebox.

Class B - This was the most popular model, which looked very much like a conventional steam locomotive. It has a horizontal boiler with cab covering the firebox, with a water tank and fuel storage space behind the cab, again all on the same frame. It had two cylinders, one on each side of the boiler, inclined at an angle of about 40° which turned a gear mechanism, which in turn transferred power to the central drive shaft and then to the axles. Whereas the A class had been largely of wooden construction, the Class B was all steel except for the wooden cab. It began with its cylinders level horizontally, but they were later dropped to the 40° angle so as to better convert the mechanical energy to the center drive shaft. They could be purchased in weights as low as 17-

This excellent action photo shows Moore Keppel Co.'s Middle Fork Railroad Climax No. 6 in operation near its Ellamore plant, hauling a log loader, in the mid-1950s. (John Krause photo, TLC Collection)

tons or as heavy as 35-tons. Most of the Climaxes used in West Virginia were of the Class B type.

Class C - These were essentially the same design as the Class B and were the largest of the Climax types, available in standard weights of 70, 80, and 90-tons. They all had three trucks, with the third truck supporting a water tender, thus keeping all engine weight on the driving wheels, just as did the 4-truck Shays.

The origin of the Climax is somewhat obscure, an early company pamphlet crediting it to a group of Pennsylvania lumbermen. It was George Gilbert of the Climax company who wrought most of the design refinements that characterized the

bulk of the production-run locomotives. The first engine was turned out in 1888 and the last in 1928.

Some variants of the type were manufactured by Dunkirk Locomotive Works, and Baldwin Locomotive Works. Both produced a few models that were very similar to the Climax except for the Climax patented devices. A few were also built by A. G. Price Ltd. in New Zealand for domestic use there.

In West Virginia the Climaxes were operated on many different lines, but they tended to be used on the smaller operations, whereas the Shays, available as heavier models were often used by the larger concerns.

Illustration from a Climax catalog of 1899 shows this neatly proportioned 35-ton locomotive. The positioning of the inclined cylinders and the central drive shaft is very evident in this very clear drawing. (TLC Collection)

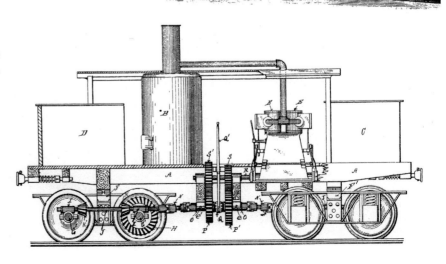

These Climax catalog illustrations show the earlier vertical boiler locomotive of the late 1880s. Note too the unusual curved gear teeth on the wheels, which allowed the drive shaft to pass above the axle and drive both axles of the truck.

This is different from the Heisler, which used straight tooth bevel gears, which require that the driving shaft and the driven shaft be in the same plane, making it impossible for the drive shaft to reach the second axle on the truck, and thus requiring the side rods that are characteristic of the Heisler.

(TLC Collection)

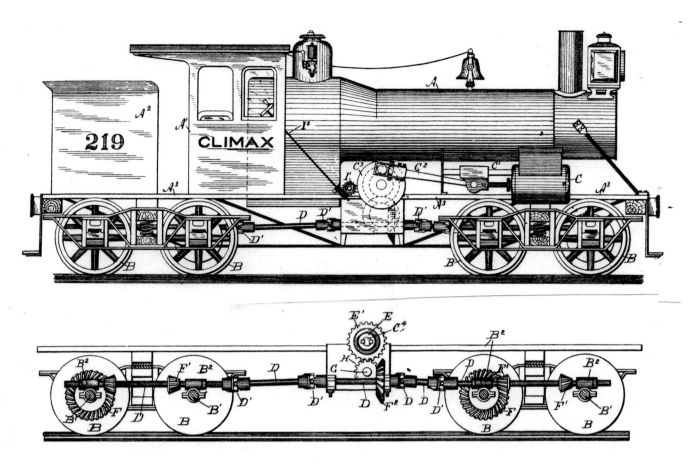

This rendering shows a Climax with its cylinders straight. Only a few were built in this way. Again, the curved teeth on the wheel gears is plainly visible. *(TLC Collection)*

This is a Climax power truck showing its makeup. In this example unusual cast steel treads on the wheels, intended for use on wooden rails or logs, were fitted. These were helpful if the logging railroad was built with wooden ties as in the illustration. (TLC Collection)

Ely-Thomas Lumber Co. Climax No. 7 is seen here stored at Jetsville in May 1955. The locomotive was later sold and placed on display in Brevard, N. C. (Richard J. Cook photo, TLC Collection)

Close-up of Climax builder's plate on W. M. Ritter Lumber Co. No. 3. (Howard W. Ameling, TLC Collection)

Elk River Coal & Lumber Co. Climax No. 3 in the woods in the mid-1950. A track gang is working behind it. Note where logs have been skidded down the hillside and are ready to be picked up. No. 3 has an interesting straight stack with circular spark arrester on top. (John Krause Photo, TLC Collection)

Elk River No. 3 is again seen fording Lilly Fork in this 1957 photo, with a single flat car. It had been out on the line to do some track work. Fording shallow streams was a characteristic of logging lines which didn't want to spend the money for bridges. It was easy to replace the track if a flood washed it out. Note the water pouring out of the underbody of the Climax. (John Krause photo, TLC Collection)

LIST OF CLIMAX LOCOMOTIVES USED IN LUMBERING OPERATIONS IN WEST VIRGINIA (62)

Owner in West Virginia	No.	Class	Gauge Inches	Weight Tons	Date Built	Constr. Number
Alexander Lbr. Co. Princeton, W. Va.	—	—	Std.	—	—	—
American Column & Lbr. Co. Ward, W. Va.		A	36	12	Prior 1910	Prior 1910
American Column & Lbr. Co. Ward, W. Va.		A	36	20	Prior 1910	Prior 1910
American Column & Lbr. Co. Colcord, W. Va.		A	42	15	Prior 1910	Prior 1910
American Column & Lbr. Co. Colcord, W. Va.		A	42	18	Prior 1910	Prior 1910
Atkins Lbr. Co. Atkins, W. Va.		B	36	25	—	—
Atkins Lbr. Co. Atkins, W. Va.		B	36	30	—	—
Atkins Lbr. Co. Atkins, W. Va.		B	36	25	—	—
Beckwith, Joel Freeport, W. Va.		A	36	12	1891	26
Blackwood Lbr. Co. Pardee, W. Va.		B	Std.	60	1909	906
Blue Jay Lbr. Co. Blue Jay, W. Va.	12	B	Std.	45	1914	1277
Blue Jay Lbr. Co. Raleigh, W. Va.	14	B	Std.	70	1920	1579?
Board Lbr. Co. Long Bottom, W. Va.	1	B?	42	Std.	—	—
Board Lbr. Co. Long Bottom, W. Va.	2	A	42	22	1924	—
Board Lbr. Co. Long Bottom, W. Va.	3	A	42	22	1926	—
Boone Tbr. Co. Clothier, W. Va.	9	B	Std.	35	1913	1223
Bowman Lbr. Co. St. Albans, W. Va.		A	42	12	—	—
Brown Lbr. Co. Piedmont, W. Va.		B	36	25	—	—
Brown, M. M. & D. D. Elkins, W. Va.		B	—	38	—	—
Buffalo Creek Lbr. Co. Rowlesburg, W. Va.	1	B	36	25	1924	—
Buffalo Creek Stave Lbr. Co. near Widen, W. Va.		A	36	Std.	—	—
Caflish Lbr. Co. Hamilton, W. Va.		B	—	38	—	—
Clay Lbr. Co. Clay County, W. Va.	2	B	Std.	25	1897-98	169
Cole & Crane Craneco, W. Va.	5	B	Std.	62	1912	—
Cole & Crane Craneco, W. Va.	6	C	Std.	85	1913	1049
Commonwealth Lbr. Co. Alderson, W. Va.	—	—	Std.	—	1906	—
Condon Lane Boom & Lbr. Co. Horton, W. Va.	4	B	Std.	25-30	1900	—
Courtney, D. G. Red House Shoals, W. Va.	—	A	60	14	1891	22
Crescent Lbr. Co. Cresmont, W. Va.	—	B	36	23	1908?	—
Croft Lbr. Co. Alexander, W. Va.	—	B	Std.	60	1916	1439
Croft Lbr. Co. Sun Crest, W. Va.	9	B	36	35	1925	—
Crosby & Beckley Algoma, W. Va.	4	B	36?	17	1898-00	—
Crosby & Beckley Algoma, W. Va.	—	B	36?	17?	1898-01	—
Crosby & Beckley Algoma, W. Va.	—	B	36?	17?	1898-01	—
Crosby & Beckley Algoma, W. Va.	—	B	36?	17?	1898-01	—
Crosby & Beckley Algoma, W. Va.	—	B	36?	17-20	1901-05	—
Crosby & Beckley Algoma, W. Va.	—	B	36?	17-20	1901-05	—
Crosby & Beckley Algoma, W. Va.	—	B	36?	17-20	1901-05	—
Crosby & Beckley Algoma, W. Va.	—	B	36?	17-20	1901-05	—
Crosby & Beckley Algoma, W. Va.	—	B	36?	17-20	1901-05	—
Dana Lbr. Co. Nada, W. Va.	2	—	Std.	—	1911	—
Delphi Lbr. Co. Cowen, W. Va.	1	B	Std.	—	1912	—
Droney, J. R. Watoga, W. Va.	4	B	Std.	42	1905-08	—
Droney, J. R. Watoga, W. Va.	2	B	Std.	35-40	—	—
East River Lbr. Co. Bluefield, W. Va.	—	A	36	15	—	—
Elk River Coal & Lbr. Co. Swandale, W. Va.	1	B	Std.	30	1916	1413
Elk River Coal & Lbr. Co. Swandale, W. Va.	2	B	Std.	50	1918	1501
Elk River Coal & Lbr. Co. Swandale, W. Va.	3	B	Std.	50	1928	1692
Elk River Coal & Lbr. Co. Swandale, W. Va.	4	C	Std.	70	1920	1579
Elk River Stave Co. Ivydale, W. Va.	—	A	36	15	—	—
Elk River Stave Co. Ivydale, W. Va.	—	B?	36	17	—	—
Ely, Ralph H., Co. Camden-on-Gauley, W. Va.	—	B	36	35	—	—
Ely-Thomas Lbr. Co. Camden-on-Gauley, W. Va.	—	B	36	35	—	—
Ely-Thomas Lbr. Co. Jetsville, W. Va.	7	B	36	35-40	1915-16	1323
Eubanks, J. J. Ojay, W. Va.	—	—	Std.	—	—	—
Gibson Lbr. Co. Masontown, W. Va.	—	A	Std.	15	1907-08	—
Glade Creek Coal & Lbr. Co. New River Valley area, W. Va.	—	B	Std.	—	—	—
Glenray Lbr. Co. Glenray, W. Va.	—	—	Std.	—	—	—
Greenbrier, Cheat & Elk R. R. Cass, W. Va.	—	B	Std.	—	1904	534
Griffith Lbr. Co. Trace, W. Va.	3	B	36	30	1925	—
Guyan Co. Fenwick (Guyan?), W. Va.	—	B	Std.	35-40	1915-17	—
Hastings, J. M., Lbr. Co. Jacksonburg, W. Va.	—	B	Std.	33	—	—
Hazens & Co. Terra Alta, W. Va.	—	A	35	12	1891	31
Henderson, Alexander Seng, W. Va.	—	A	36	12	1891	28
Himmelrech, W. H., Lbr. Co. Belington, W. Va.	—	B	Std.	25	1894-97	—
Hutchinson Lbr. Co. Huntington, W. Va.	1	B	36	30	1918	—
Interstate Cooperage Co. Shock, W. Va.	11	B	36	—	1927	—
Kellys Creek Lbr. Co. ———, W. Va.	—	A	Std.	15	—	—
Kendall Lbr. Co. Cheat Haven, W. Va.	—	B	36	25	1895-97	—
Keys Fannin Lbr. Co. Herndon, W. Va.	—	B	36	20	1901?	—
Keys Fannin Lbr. Co. Herndon, W. Va.	—	B	36	20	1901?	—
Leatherwood Lbr. Co. Altman (or Morroco), W. Va.	3	B	Std.	52	1911	1127
Leatherwood Lbr. Co. Altman (or Morroco), W. Va.	—	B	Std.	25	—	—
Leatherwood Lbr. Co. Altman (or Morroco), W. Va.	—	B	Std.	30	—	—
Lewis Bros. Lbr. Co. Glady, W. Va.	—	B	N.G.?	—	—	—
Logan Planing Mills Co. Logan, W. Va.	—	B	Std.	35	1926	—
Logan Planing Mills Co. Logan, W. Va.	—	B	Std.	35	—	—
Maryland Lbr. Co. Denmar, W. Va.	—	B	Std.	42	—	—
Mason, W. H., Lbr. Co. Elkins, W. Va.	—	B	Std.	40	1913	1237
Miller, A. V. Nida, W. Va.	—	—	42	20	—	—
Moore-Keppel & Co. Ellamore, W. Va.	1	B	Std.	35	1906	678
Moore-Keppel & Co. Ellamore, W. Va.	2	B	Std.	35	1909	930
Moore-Keppel & Co. Ellamore, W. Va.	3	B	Std.	50-55	1910	1059
Moore-Keppel & Co. Ellamore, W. Va.	4	B	Std.	40	1913	1237
Moore-Keppel & Co. Ellamore, W. Va.	5	B	Std.	60	1916	1399
Moore-Keppel & Co. Ellamore, W. Va.	6	C	Std.	70	1919	1551

Company / Location	No.	Class	Gauge	Wt.	Year	C/N
Morrison & Gross, near Davis?, W. Va.	—	B	Std.	—	—	—
Mountain State Lbr. Co. ————, W. Va.	—	B	36	25	1924	—
New Moorefield Lbr. Co. Moorefield, W. Va.	—	—	36	—	—	—
New River Lbr. Co. Longbottom, W. Va.	1	B	42	—	—	—
New River Lbr. Co. Longbottom, W. Va.	2	A	42	22	1924	—
New River Lbr. Co. Longbottom, W. Va.	3	A	42	22	1926	—
New River Lbr. Co. Longbottom, W. Va.	4	B	42	35	1927	—
Pardee & Curtin Lbr. Co. Curtin, W. Va.	6	—	Std.	—	—	—
Peytona Lbr. Co. Peytona, W. Va.	—	—	Std.	—	1907	—
Peytona Lbr. Co. Christian, W. Va.	—	—	36	—	—	—
Peytona Lbr. Co. Christian, W. Va.	—	—	36	—	—	—
Pocahontas R. R. Boyer, W. Va.	8	B	Std.	45-50	1918-19	—
Pocahontas Central R. R. of W. Va. Harter, W. Va.	1	B	N.G.	20	1906-10	—
Porter Lbr. Co. ————, W. Va.	—	B				
Rinard, S. Cranesville, W. Va.	—	A	60	13	1891	21
Ritter, C. L., Lbr. Co. Clay, W. Va.	—	B?	42	17	—	—
Ritter, C. L., Lbr. Co. Clay, W. Va.	—	B?	42	17	—	—
Ritter, W. M., Lbr. Co. Hurley, W. Va.	180	B	Std.	17	1898	180
Ritter, W. M., Lbr. Co. Hurley, W. Va.	206	B	Std.	—	—	206
Ritter, W. M., Lbr. Co. Hurley, W. Va.	217	B	Std.	25	1900	217
Ritter, W. M., Lbr. Co. Hurley, W. Va.	247	B	Std.	—	—	247
Ritter, W. M., Lbr. Co. Hurley, W. Va.	—	B	42	17	1898-00	—
Rockcastle Lbr. Co. Seth, W. Va.	—	—	Std.	—	1913?	—
Ruthbell Lbr. Co. Elkins, W. Va.	—	A	36	18	—	—
Sharpnack Lbr. Co. Huntington, W. Va.	—	A?	36?	—	—	—
South Fork Lbr. Co. Moorefield, W. Va.	1	B	42	35	1915-19	—
South Fork Lbr. Co. Moorefield, W. Va.	2	B	42	35	1912-22	—
Spice Run Lbr. Co. Locust, W. Va.	5	C	Std.	70	1920	1579?
Tomb Lbr. Co. Watoga, W. Va.	4	B	Std.	42	1905-08	—
Tomb Lbr. Co. Watoga, W. Va.	2	B	—	35-40	—	—
West Virginia Hardwood Lbr. Co. Jack, W. Va.	153	B	Std.	20	1897	153
West Virginia Hardwood Lbr. Co. Jack, W. Va.	—	B	Std.	20	1895	—
West Virginia Hardwood Lbr. Co. Jack, W. Va.	—	A	Std.	10	1896	—
West Virginia Pulp & Paper Co. Dobbins, W. Va.	1	—	Std.	—	1904	534
West Virginia Tbr. Co. Vaughn, W. Va.	—	B?	36	—	1915	—
West Virginia Tbr. Co. Vaughn, W. Va.	—	A?	36	—	—	—
West Virginia Tbr. Co. Vaughn, W. Va.	—	A	36	—	—	—
West Virginia Tbr. Co. Vaughn, W. Va.	—	A	36	—	—	—
West Virginia Tbr. Co. Vaughn, W. Va.	—	A	36	—	—	—
Wheeler Lbr. Co. Glady, W. Va.	1	B	Std.	45	1910	—

This roster is taken from *Tumult on the Mountain* by Roy B. Clarckson and used with permission of McClain Printing Co., Parsons, W.Va.

Elk River No. 3 on May 31, 1958. This view shows the rear of the locomotive a little better than most photos. Unusually for a Climax in West Virginia, this engine is equipped with Walschaerts valve gear, evident by all the extra rods on the cylinders and flywheel, rather than the more common Stephenson valve gear. (TLC Collection)

It might well be said that the Heisler was the "also ran" in the geared locomotive race. It ran a poor third to Shays and Climaxes, and gained very little acceptance in West Virginia or in the Appalachian logging region overall.

There were about 625 Heislers built in the period 1891 to 1941. Of this number a scant 13 were used new in West Virginia.

The Heisler was designed by Charles L. Heisler, an Ohio-born man who went to work for the Brooks Locomotive Works in Dunkirk, New York, in the late 1880s, and while there developed his design for a geared locomotive. Like the Climax, his engine had a central drive shaft (whereas the Shay's was offset on the right side). The cylinders were arranged in a "V" shape beneath the boiler. They applied their power to a mechanism that transmitted it to the drive shaft and subsequently to the trucks. Unlike the Climax and Shay, only one axle of each truck was powered. A connecting rod, very evident in photos, drove the second axle of each truck. A single engine was built at Dunkirk, then Heisler resigned and left, with his patent, since Brooks and Dunkirk Engineering Co., an associated subsidiary, didn't want to build the type. He approached Baldwin Locomotive Works and though Baldwin didn't take up the work, the Heisler patent was licensed to Stearns Manufacturing Company of Erie, Pa. This company was closely aligned with Baldwin and was already a builder of sawmill equipment and power plants. The addition of the geared locomotive fit its business well, since it was already selling widely within the logging/lumbering industry.

Stearns built the new Heislers, but because of the economic depression of 1893 wasn't highly successful at first. According to Benjamin Klein in his book *The Heisler Locomotive*, the fact that the locomotive was offered only in one size was also a drawback. Eventually the company began to offer a number of different sizes, all having two trucks, including 14, 20, 25, 30 and 45-ton varieties. The first engines were very successful and the Stearns Company continued building them until it was dissolved in 1905. After that the Heislers were manufactured by the Heisler Locomotive Works of Erie, with the locomotive as its sole product. It continued to produce the type until 1941. In 1922 the largest type of Heisler was added to the line, a three-truck 70-ton design, which had a water tender with a powered truck under it in the same manner as some 3-truck Shays and Climaxes.

Klein, in his book, concludes that the Heislers had wide popularity in the Southeastern U. S., where they could be used in fairly level territory that was swampy and wet. They seemed to perform very well in this environment. They were also widely used in the western U. S., but gained little acceptance in the Appalachian logging region. He has no explanation for this lack of interest on the part of the loggers working the eastern mountains, nor do we. Certainly the engines met very good performance standards and usually got high marks from their owners.

One thing that set the Heisler apart was that its gears were enclosed in a box which kept them bathed in lubricant. The Shay and Climax both had exposed gears which were susceptible to ingesting snow, ice, grime, and debris, all of which tended to wear out the gearing. This was apparently another reason Heislers had wide acceptance in wet areas.

Heislers were popular also with contractors involved in large earth-moving projects, as well as industries requiring in-house switching, to a much greater degree than the Shay and Climax.

Heisler No. 7 of Moore Keppel's Middle Fork Railroad is seen here hauling hopper and box cars near Ellamore in the mid-1950s. The pleasing proportions of the locomotive are evident here, including its straight stack made possible by the spark arrester being in the smoke box. Note the characteristic spoked wheels with connecting rods. (John Krause Photo, TLC Collection)

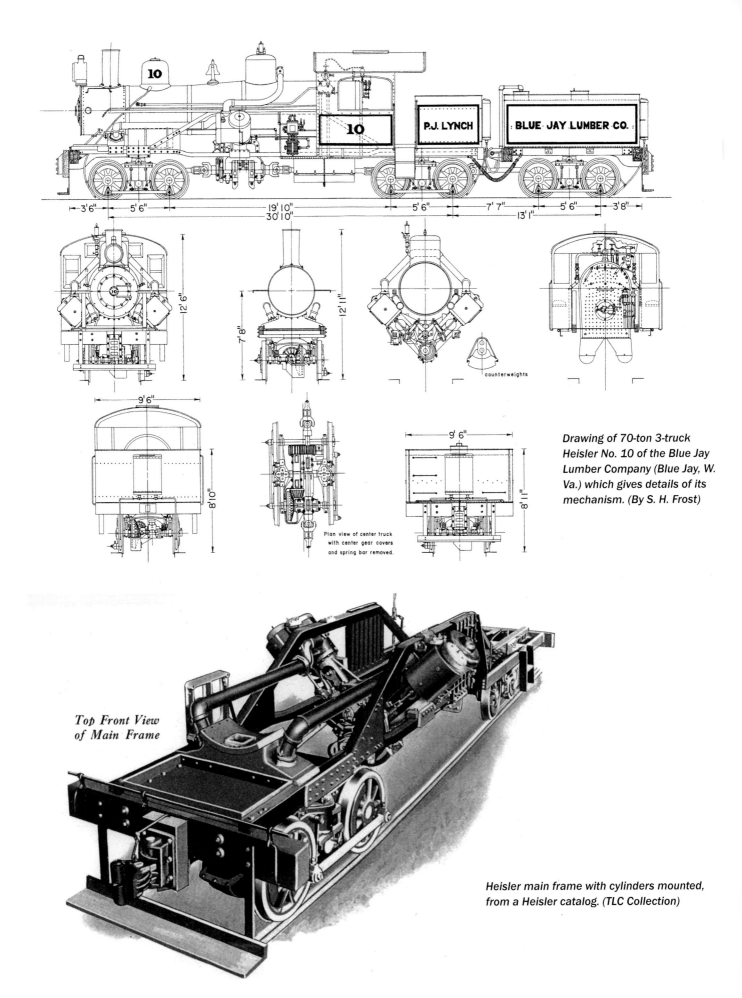

10

10   P.J. LYNCH   BLUE JAY LUMBER CO.

3'6" 5'6"   19'10"   5'6"   7'7"   5'6"   3'8"
            30'10"   13'1"

12'6"

7'8"   12'11"

counterweights

9'6"

8'10"

Plan view of center truck
with center gear covers
and spring bar removed.

9'6"

8'11"

*Drawing of 70-ton 3-truck
Heisler No. 10 of the Blue Jay
Lumber Company (Blue Jay, W.
Va.) which gives details of its
mechanism. (By S. H. Frost)*

*Top Front View
of Main Frame*

*Heisler main frame with cylinders mounted,
from a Heisler catalog. (TLC Collection)*

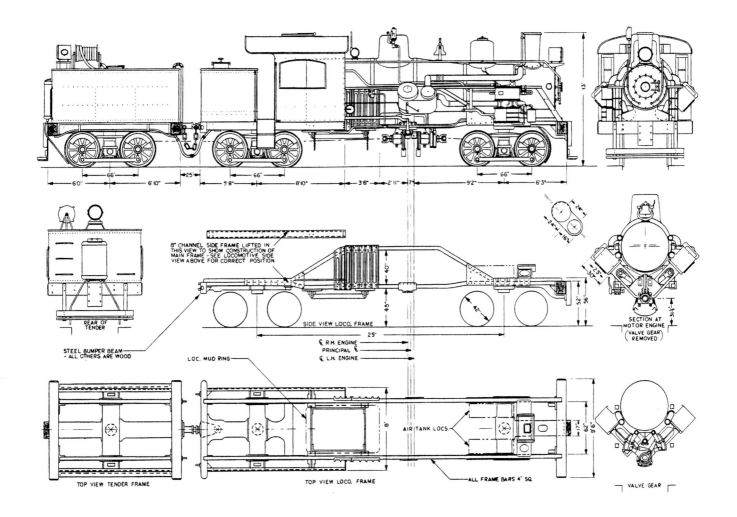

This drawing shows a typical 3-truck Heisler including its frame and cylinder placement. (TLC Collection)

Detail of cylinders, sitting in their V formation, from a Heisler catalog. (TLC Collection)

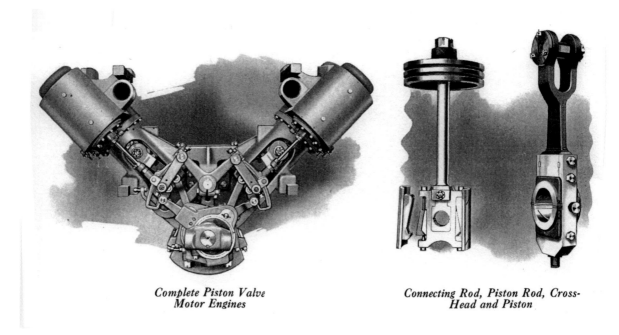

Complete Piston Valve Motor Engines

Connecting Rod, Piston Rod, Cross-Head and Piston

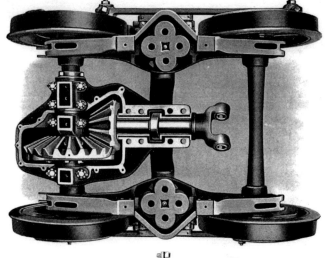

Plan, side and end view of a Heisler truck, showing how the gears were arranged. Unique to the geared engine design, Heislers powered only one axle on each truck, supplying power to the second by way of a side rod. From a Heisler catalog. (TLC Collection)

Plan view of trucks with spring bar, gear cover and pinion shaft caps removed. Gears and thrust collar of pinion shafts run in oil, fully enclosed

Side view of trucks all assembled showing flexibility which enables drivers to independently adapt themselves to high or low spots in the rail without changing relation of gears or straining driving mechanism

End view of trucks all assembled Note flexible connection between gear case and Swivel bar

This Heisler catalog illustration illustrates very clearly the overall design composition of the type. This particular 3-truck 80-ton locomotive burned coal, but most Heislers (as well as Shays and Climaxes) used wood, for obvious reasons. (TLC Collection)

LIST OF HEISLER LOCOMOTIVES USED IN LUMBERING OPERATIONS IN WEST VIRGINIA (217)

Owner in West Virginia	No.	Gauge Inches	Weight Tons	Constr. Number
Blue Jay Lbr. Co. Blue Jay, W Va.	10	Std.	78	1252
Chemical & Helvetia R. R Selbyville, W. Va.	1	36	32	1279
Chemical & Helvetia R. R. Selbyville, W. Va.	2	36	32	1348
Kendall Lbr. Co. Cheat Haven, Penn.	—	Std.	85	1376
Lamb-Fish Lbr. Co. Charleston, W. Va.	—	Std.	36	1260
Mayton Lbr. Co. Pickens, W. Va. (also owned by Ralph H. Ely, Frenchton, W. Va.)	4	36	34	1271
Meadow River Lbr. Co. Rainelle, W. Va.	6	Std.	90	1591
Middle Fork R. R. Ellamore, W. Va.	7	Std.	90	1607
Morrison & Gross & Co Wallman, Md.	—	36	24	1511
Oakland Lbr. Co. Orgas, W. Va.	—	36	32	1490
Potomac Lbr. Co. McNeil, W. Va.	—	Std.	20	1089
Range Lbr. Co. Deer Creek, W. Va.	—	Std.	37	1011
West Virginia Midland R. R. Palmer, W. Va. (also owned by Pardee-Curtin Lbr. Co. Curtin, W. Va.)	—	36	3	1173

This roster is taken from *Tumult on the Mountain* by Roy B. Clarckson and used with permission of McClain Printing Co., Parsons, W.Va.

Portrait of a Heisler. Meadow River No. 6 rests on a sunny afternoon in November 1961 outside the engine house at the big mill in Rainelle. (W. E. Warden photo, TLC Collection)

This chapter is an album of photos showing the Shay type of geared locomotive at work on West Virginia logging railroads. More photos of Shays at work in West Virginia have survived than Climaxes, regardless of the fact that there were also a large number of Climaxes that worked in the state. It is not surprising that they far outnumber Heislers, since so few of the latter were used. Part of this may be that the Shays were used by the largest and the longest lasting of the logging companies and thus were at work later than the Climaxes, affording people a better chance to take photos of them, especially in the last decade or two when railfans were out doing photography. The photos in this chapter are randomly selected, the main aim being to demonstrate the widest possible variety of locomotives in the most diverse settings. They are not necessarily arranged in any geographical order or chronological context.

Today, the Shay is seen as the preeminent example of the geared logging locomotive and most of the geared engines that survive today and are displayed or used in active service on tourist lines are Shays. One of the best aggregation of Shays is at the Cass Scenic Railroad state park at Cass, in Pocahontas County, West Virginia. Included in this collection is the giant Western Maryland No. 6, which was never used for logging but rather was for carrying coal to and from a mine at the end of WM's Chaffee Branch in West Virginia and Maryland. It is the final refinement of the type, being the last and largest Shay built, in 1945.

Included in this chapter are brief sidebars about the large Shays that were used by the class I railroads of the state, the C&O with its largest-ever fleet for a Class I railroad, as well as the WM's Chaffee Branch Shays and the single N&W type.

Shays were well liked by most timber operators not only for their excellent capabilities but also because they could be sold off easily to other operators as a result of their high reputation for efficiency and reliability as well as ease of maintenance, especially compared with the Heislers. Their reputation was very high, and remains so in the retrospect of historical inquiry.

Diagram of a large 3-truck Shay with the various parts labeled

1 Cylinder	6 Right Truck Box Cap	11 Crank Shaft	16 Truss Rod End, Front
2 Exhaust Pipe	7 Gear	12 Crank Box Cap	17 Reverse Lever Shaft Arm
3 Exhaust Pipe Elbow	8 Coupling Ring	13 Cylinder Frame	18 Coal Bunk
4 Exhaust Reducer	9 Square Shaft	14 Tumbling Shaft	19 Water Tank
5 Line Shaft	10 Sleeve Coupling	15 Truss Rod End, Back	20 Rear Sand Box

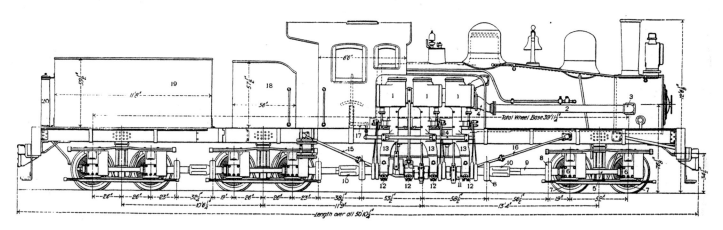

Opposite: Mower Lumber Company Shay No. 4 is heading a long train loading on the line up the mountain out of Cass in 1955. Right behind the train is a pile of logs that have been skidded out of the woods to a point of loading on the railroad. Note that the rail bed is well laid with good sawn ties and fairly good rails, not always the case on logging lines. (John Krause Photo, TLC Collection)

Meadow River Lumber Company, headquartered out of Rainelle, liked the balloon style stacks on its logging engines. Here Shays 5 and 3 are on the line north of Anjean in the summer of 1956. No. 3 has just arrived with some machinists to work on No. 5, which was having a mechanical problem. Meadow River was a high class operation, even having ex-C&O cabooses. Its product was shipped via the NF&G to C&O mainline at Meadow Creek. (John Krause photo, TLC Collection)

Note that this Meadow River train, powered by No. 7, has a caboose for a track crew and a flat car loaded with ties for use in track laying north of Anjean. The flat car isn't a logging car but a borrowed C&O flat. (D. Wallace Johnson photo)

Opposite: Ely-Thomas Lumber Company Shays No. 2 and 6 illustrate the most common of the spark arrester stacks used on Shay, the diamond shape. Other types were used, but this was by far the most common, and the one that Lima usually fitted to new Shays. No. 2 is near Fenwick in about 1960, fairly late in the steam logging era. No. 6 is a narrow gauge engine. Ely-Thomas had both standard and narrow gauge lines and locomotives. Its outside connection was via the Baltimore & Ohio. (C&O Historical Society Collection (CSPR-5263), and Harold K. Vollrath Collection, respectively)

No. 7, another of Meadow River's balloon-stacked Shays is parked in this mid-1950s scene at the big mill at Rainelle. (John Krause photo, TLC Collection)

A good ¾ view of Meadow River No. 1 at Rainelle on May 26, 1956. (W. A. Swartz photo, TLC Collection)

At Alexander, W. Va., Croft Lumber Company Shay No. 5 is seen here with some camp cars ready to head for the woods to put them down for the loggers to use. Note that it has its spark arrester in the smoke box, therefore has a straight stack. (TLC Collection)

Parsons Lumber Company No. 8, a snazzy looking 3-truck locomotive painted like a mainline engine, also sports the straight stack. (TLC Collection)

Another photo of a Croft Lumber Company Shay shows it with a varied train having logs, log loader, box car (supplies for the woods probably), more logs and a caboose of some kind. Another straight stacked engine. (TLC Collection)

Another scene on the Parsons Lumber Company line, No. 7 a two-trucker has a log loader and some logs. Note the link-and-pin couplers with no less than three different level pockets (TLC Collection)

This is an example of a very small Shay, just two cylinders, on the A. G. Miller Lumber Company line at Nida, W. Va. The men almost dwarf this small engine. (Pocahontas Co. Historical Society Collection)

Opposite Top: In this interesting woods scene a balloon stacked Shay and its log loader is placing a logger's shack preparatory to some operations in this "neck of the woods." Unfortunately, we don't have a date or location for this photo. (TLC Collection)

Opposite Bottom: This is a great woods scene showing Glady Fork Lumber Company (Glady, W. Va.) two-truck Shay powering a train with a log loader caught in the act of hoisting a log. The track laid on the flat cars is certainly evident here. This is another straight-stacked locomotive. What appears to be a log holding pond is in the foreground. (TLC Collection)

Another small locomotive, a two-truck Shay with its three cylinders on an angle rather than vertical as on bigger engines, indicating that this engine was probably originally built as a narrow gauge engine, and later rebuilt to standard gauge. This is on the Hoover-Yaeger Lumber Company line out of Durbin. (TLC Collection)

These two photos show Shays 1 and 2 of the A. D. Neil Company in Pocahontas County, with log trains:
Above: Crew poses for a photo beside No. 1 with its unusual conical spark arrester screen.
Below: No. 2 with its conical screen tipped open has just loaded logs. Note the horses which have been used to skid the logs to the loader.
(Both TLC Collection)

This two-truck Shay of the Orwig, Kyder & Co. line near Boyer, W. Va., in Pocahontas County, has two giant oil headlights. Other interesting aspects of the scene are the horses with logs which here are being slid along skids onto the cars. We don't know the exact purpose of the wooden sluice in the background, but it has a gondola car at the bottom. (Pocahontas County Historical Society Collection)

This angle shows this Campbell Lumber Company (of Marlinton) three truck Shay of powerful proportions with some good sized logs in tow. (TLC Collection)

North Fork Lumber Company, out of Boyer, W. Va. (connecting with the C&O's Greenbrier Branch) rostered this two-truck Shay sometime about 1910. Note the pole inserted in the front coupler pocket, which was used to push cars on adjacent tracks. (TCL Collection)

A Pocahontas Lumber Company Shay has come to grief in this scene. It's a good thing that the engine has almost made it to the shore before the trestle collapsed. (TCL Collection)

This is an unusual scene. . . A doubleheaded log train. Two Shays of the Pocahontas Lumber Company (of Burner, W. Va.) has its train stopped at a huge pile of logs. (TLC Collection)

Parsons Pulp and Paper Company Shay No. 1 in Tucker County with its train in about 1910. Chains similar to that on the locomotive appear to be the stays holding the logs on the cars. They don't look that secure! (TLC Collection)

This nice clean Shay with angled cylinders at tall capped stack belonged to the Blue Jay Lumber Company, connecting with C&O in Raleigh County is seen here with a C&O box car probably loaded with provisions for the company. (Courtesy Sallie Williams)

This is the instance of the use of a Shay on a road that largely carried coal. The narrow gauge Mann's Creek Railroad carried coal from its mine high above the new River Gorge, down to the C&O connection at Sewell where coke ovens converted the coal to coke before shipment. This outsized balloon stack is the hallmark on this nice looking Shay. (H. K. Vollrath Collection)

In 1900 West Virginia Pulp and Paper Company began its huge operations at Cass, as the C&O built its Greenbrier Subdivision up that river to Cass and beyond just to serve this and the many other mills that were soon in operation along the line. Shay No. 10 is seen here about 1920 along the Slay Fork with the stylish capped water tank in the background. (West Virginia Collection, West Virginia University)

Look at the huge pile of logs at this location as Shay No. 3 of West Virginia Pulp and Paper Company's "Greenbrier Cheat & Elk Railroad" pauses with a log loader to pick up a few of these in the ca. 1910 era. (West Virginia Collection, West Virginia University)

Greenbrier Cheat & Elk Shay No. 5 is about to negotiate the "Upper Switchback" on its way down the mountain to the mill at Cass in 1909. This switchback is still used by tourist trains on the Cass Scenic Railroad today. (TLC Collection)

The log cribbing of the bridge is one of the prominent features in this scene as a Greenbrier Cheat & Elk Shay takes a big trainload of logs toward the mill in the early part of the 20th Century. (TLC Collection)

The engineer is "oiling around" Mower Lumber Company No. 4 on the mountain out of Cass in the mid-1950s. Mower was the successor to West Virginia Pulp and Paper (WVaP&P), which in turn was a successor to the Greenbrier, Cheat, and Elk (GC&E). All steam locomotives needed a great deal of lubrication, and Shays even more because of their complicated gearing. Often 5-gallon tin cans of grease and oil can be seen carried on the running board for such use. (John Krause photo, TLC Collection)

A Mower Lumber Co. Shay, on its way up the mountain from Cass in the mid-1950s has derailed and the crew is using blocks of wood to get it back on the track. Scenes such as this were a more-often-than-not experienced on many poorly laid logging roads; less so on well built and established line like Mower. (John Krause photo, TLC Collection)

In the mid-1950s Mower Shay No. 4 pushes empty log flat at "Gum Field" on the mountain out of Cass. Today the riders on the Cass Scenic Railroad tourist line are treated to great mountain scenery at this location, just before they reach the first station on the tourist line at Whitaker. (John Krause photo, TLC Collection)

Supplies are arriving at Mower Lumber Company log camp in this 1960 photo. Note the 55-gallon drum of oil next to the portable building, a necessity for use in oiling the locomotives, skidders, and other machinery used in logging. The line would be abandoned just a few years after this photo. The man in the center holding the two sacks is photographer John Krause. (John Krause photo, TLC Collection)

This slightly elevated view of Mower #4 gives a nice perspective of the top of the locomotive as it switches this location in October 1957. (John Krause photo, TLC Collection)

On a pleasant summer day in September 1962, Ely-Thomas Shays 2 and 3 sit at the Fenwick yard awaiting assignment. (W. E. Warden photo, TLC Collection)

This rear view of Ely-Thomas No. 2 at Fenwick in 1960 gives us a good view of the rear of the water tender's arrangement. Note in particular the two sandboxes on the back of the tender. (TLC Collection)

Cherry River Boom and Lumber Company, headquartered at Richwood, W. Va. (where connection was made with B&O), was one of the largest and longest lasting of West Virginia's lumber operations. It used both rod (see p.27) and geared locomotives. Here Shay No. 7 and its crew wait for another train to pass on the left in 1956. (William E. Arden photo, TLC Collection)

Cherry River Shay 7 is headed for the woods and logs with its train of flats in the mid-1950s near Blizzard Run. (John Krause photo, TLC Collection)

W. M. Ritter Lumber No. 19 Shay in bright light in the late afternoon sun in September 1959, displaying its gearing quite starkly. (David G. Knox photo, TLC Collection)

Ritter Shay No. 12 is seen here stored and out of service amid the clutter of machinery at the Swandale mill in March 1960, behind it rests the hulk of Climax No. 3. At right, still lettered Elk River Coal & Lumber is the tank of Climax 3. (William E. Warden photo, TLC Collection)

Elk River diesel with a log loader is seen here passing a Shay with a "For Sale" sign hung on the smokebox. Logging railroads didn't last long enough to use a lot of diesels to replace steam. (TLC Collection)

The crew of Elk River Coal & Lumber No. 19 wait for a Buffalo Creek & Gauley train to pass on the main line at Avca before they go on to the mill at Swandale. Note the 5-gallon cans of grease on the running board, a big part of keeping the Shays in operation.

Repairs out in the woods were often necessary. Here a machinist is working with the air pump of Elk River Coal and Lumber Shay 19 in the 1950s. (TLC Collection)

Elk River No. 12 is seen here fording a stream. Note that its log flats are high class steel cars unlike many of the smaller and earlier operations which used rickety wooden cars or just separate bogey trucks without a frame. (John Krause photo, TLC Collection)

Opposite Top: After getting its repairs, No. 19 went on to siphon up some water at Lilley Fork. (TLC Collection)

Opposite Below: A wonderful scene showing a perfectly composed log train. Elk River Shay No. 12 with five loads of logs and a 4-wheel bobber caboose in the mid-1950s. (John Krause photo, TLC Collection)

This photo was taken of a Mower Lumber Company Shay on the last day that logging runs were made up Back Alleghany Mountain near Gum Field in August 1960. (John Krause photo, TLC Collection)

Opposite Top: Elk River Shay 19 is in the foreground here as No. 12 works in the distance at Swandale in the early 1950s. (John Krause photo, TLC Collection)

Opposite Bottom: Ritter Shay No. 19, actually being operated by Georgia Pacific after its takeover, but still lettered Ritter, is seen in a blinding snow storm in December 1960 near Swandale. This must have been what it was like on so many harsh winter days in the late 19th and early 20th Century years of very cold winters. (John Killoran photo, TLC Collection)

Shays on Class I Railroads in West Virginia

Three of the major Class I railroads serving West Virginia owned Shay locomotives. This is quite unusual as there were only two or three other Class I railroads in the United States which owned Shays, and only one of these bought them new. The Chesapeake & Ohio comes in first with a huge roster of 16 locomotives, Western Maryland is next with five, and Norfolk & Western is last at one lone locomotive. None of them lasted to modern times except the WM engines, most especially WM No. 6, the heaviest, most powerful, and all round biggest Shay ever constructed as well as the very last.

Western Maryland

WM started experimenting with its first Shay, getting its No. 900 in June 1906. It was a huge 150-ton locomotive and was intended for use on some of the steepest coal branches and also on the mainline in steep territory such as the Black Fork grade, but it was sold to a Mexican concern by 1910.

When WM acquired the steep Chaffee Branch from the Chaffee Coal Company in 1929, it received with it Chaffee's Shay which became WM No. 4 (lasting on the roster until 1945). Sometime in the 1920s WM also got a Shay from the Greenbrier Cheat & Elk RR, which it gave road number 3, but it was retired in 1932, and sold, subsequently serving on several logging lines.

It was after the acquisition of the Chaffee Branch in 1929 that WM concentrated its two Shays on that line. It ran between Chaffee, West Virginia and Vindex, Maryland, the location of several productive mines. The grades on this line ran as high as nearly 10%. Luckily the coal loads were hauled downgrade, but tremendous effort was still needed just to lift the empty hoppers up to the mine.

For some reason in the 1940s, WM decided to supplement its one remaining Shay with another. In May 1945 Lima delivered WM 6, which was the last Shay ever built.

No. 6 weighed 324,000 pounds, exerted 59,740 pounds of attractive effort, resting on three trucks an measuring 66 feet and ½ inch over the coupler faces. It was of the three truck design with the third truck under the water tender. The cylinders were mounted independently of the boiler on heavy girders frames.

The Chaffee Branch's last mine was closed in 1950, and No. 6 was kept until 1954 when it donated to the B&O Railroad Museum and remained there until 1980 when it was transferred to the Cass Scenic Railroad, where it operates today.

This profile of the Chaffee Branch shows why the Western Maryland used Shays – the grade was far in excess of what railroads could normally operate with rod engines. (TLC Collection)

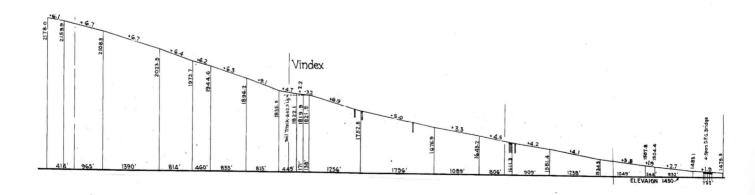

WM Shay No. 6, the last and largest of the WM Shays, is seen at Vindex, Md. on August 19, 1946, shortly after it arrived new from the Lima Locomotive Works. (TLC Collection)

Shay No. 6 is seen here with a train of coal. It remained in this service through 1953. Later it rested for many years in the B&O Railroad Museum in Baltimore, and today it is famous as one of the Shays operated on West Virginia's Cass Scenic Railroad State Park. (TLC Collection)

No. 6 is switching at the Mauar Mine #1 near Vindex, Md. on the Chaffee Branch in 1946. The branch connected with the WM main line just across the border in West Virginia. (C.W. Jernstrom photo, TLC Collection)

Although the big Shay No. 6 got all the attention, publicity, and interest, WM had four others, two of which were used into the 1940s and 1950s. No. 5 was purchased by the WM from the Greenbrier, Cheat, and Elk logging line at Cass, who had purchased it from the C&O. Built in 1910, it was retired, along with No. 6, in 1953-54. This photo was taken at Ridgely in the 1940s. (Jay Williams Collection)

Elevation and sections of WM No. 6 from Railway Mechanical Engineer, December 1945.

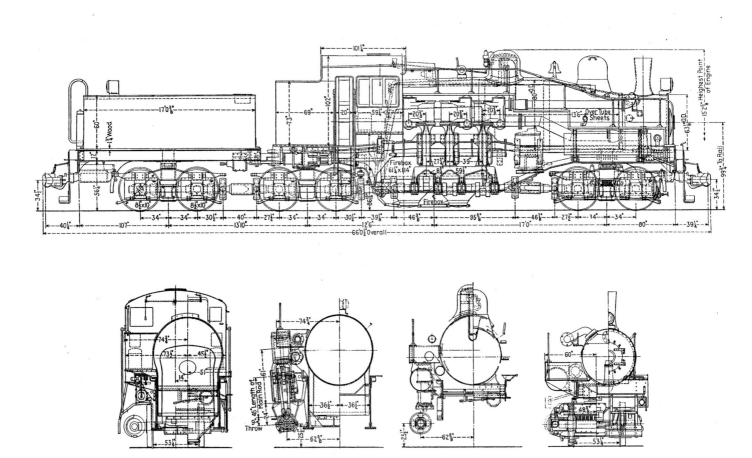

WM No. 900, the first WM Shay, is seen here soon after arrival, pushing a train up the Black Fork grade at Tub Run. (TLC Collection)

WM Shay No. 3 (ex-Greenbrier Cheat & Elk No. 7) shifting hoppers at a small mine tipple. (TLC Collection)

Norfolk & Western

N&W had one Shay, its No. 56, built by Lima in 1907. It was a 150-ton 4-truck design. Apparently it was purchased for use on some of the steeper lines between Bluefield and Williamson, West Virginia. It remained on the roster only until 1915 when it was sold to the Birmingham Locomotive & Car Company, and subsequent to that was used the Red River RR in California, which retired it in 1934.

It was obvious that N&W had no real place for geared locomotives in its operations. In fact N&W did own four other Shays and one Climax which came to it when it acquired the 42-inch gauge Big Sandy & Cumberland Railroad between Devon, West Virginia, and Grundy, Virginia. This route was standard gauged and became the basis for N&W's Buchanan Branch. The locomotives were not retained.

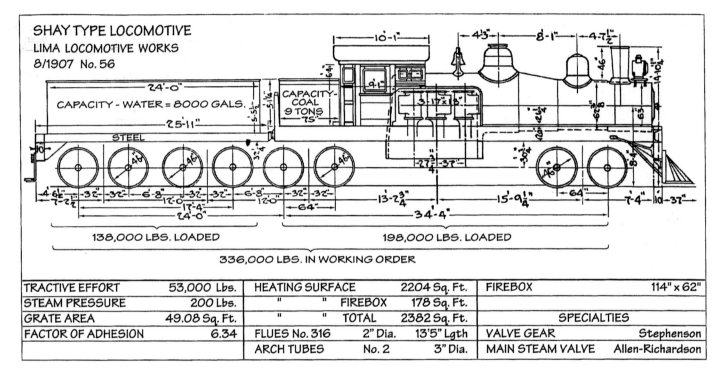

SHAY TYPE LOCOMOTIVE
LIMA LOCOMOTIVE WORKS
8/1907 No. 56

CAPACITY - WATER = 8000 GALS.

CAPACITY COAL 9 TONS

138,000 LBS. LOADED   198,000 LBS. LOADED

336,000 LBS. IN WORKING ORDER

TRACTIVE EFFORT	53,000 Lbs.	HEATING SURFACE			2204 Sq. Ft.	FIREBOX		114" x 62"
STEAM PRESSURE	200 Lbs.	"	"	FIREBOX	178 Sq. Ft.			
GRATE AREA	49.08 Sq. Ft.	"	"	TOTAL	2382 Sq. Ft.	SPECIALTIES		
FACTOR OF ADHESION	6.34	FLUES No. 316	2" Dia.	13'5" Lgth		VALVE GEAR		Stephenson
		ARCH TUBES		No. 2	3" Dia.	MAIN STEAM VALVE		Allen-Richardson

This is an N&W diagram showing Shay No. 56 (N&W Historical Society)

Lima builder's photo of N&W Shay No. 56. (Harold K. Volrath Collection)

Chesapeake & Ohio

C&O was the largest owner of Shay locomotives among Class I railroads, but they lasted only a short while. The railway decided to acquire its first Shays for the steep 4.6% grade Keeney's Creek Branch off the New River Subdivision. It acquired No. 7, a 4-truck 150-ton Shay that weighed in at 323,650 pounds, among the heaviest ever built. With some success with this locomotive after its arrival in 1906, additional Shays were purchased for use on the Rend Subdivision out of Thurmond, not far from Keeney's Creek, and on the Laurel Creek Branch out of Quinnimont, another New River Subdivision branch with heavy grades. The locomotives were also used on the Seng Creek line between the Cabin Creek and Paint Creek Subdivisions. With the building of new lines and availability of rod locomotives capable of the job, C&O decided to get rid of the odd locomotives and by 1924 had sold them all.

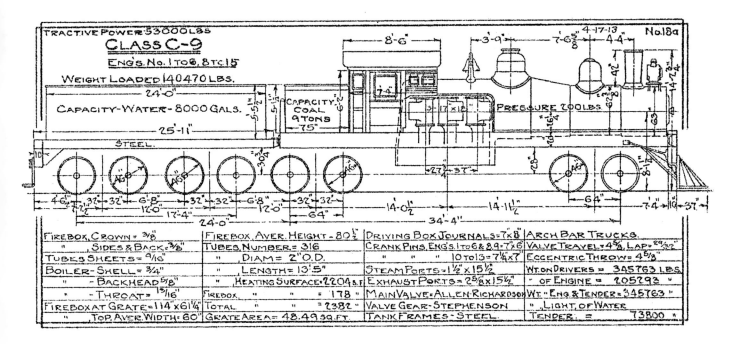

C&O Diagram of giant 4-Truck No. 7. (C&O Historical Society Collection)

C&O Shay No. 6 on the Keeney's Creek Subdivision circa 1910. (C&O Historical Society Collection)

C&O Shay No. 6 at Thurmond circa 1915, where it was used on the Rend Subdivision just across the New River. From an old post card. (C.E. Armstrong photo, C&O Historical Society Collection)

Three-truck C&O Shay No. 16 at Thurmond during its stint of duty on the steep Rend Subdivision out of that New River Gorge town. (C&O Historical Society Collection)

This chapter depicts the Climax type of geared engine in the forests of West Virginia as revealed in available photography. Although the number of Climaxes bought new almost equaled the number of Shays in West Virginia, fewer photos have survived showing them. This may be that the Climax types tended to be used by the smaller, more obscure loggers and were also gone sooner than the Shays. Although the Climax was a well-liked type it appeared usually in smaller sizes (weights) and power than did Shays overall. This more or less suited the type to the smaller logging lines and operations.

When railfans began looking for logging railroads to photograph in the 1950s, they tended toward the larger operations with Shays, so fewer Climax photos are extant today. It also appears, at least from available resources, that by the early 1950s, when the logging railroads were in their last years, most of the Climaxes were gone.

The Climax was a reliable, efficient, and well-liked machine which did its job very well in West Virginia as well as other parts of the country where it was used. It could be maintained by shop forces in the machine shops of lumber companies/railroads, and was reliable to a high degree in the work for which it was intended.

The Climax presents an appearance that looks a bit more like a regular rod locomotive in that it has two cylinders on each side of a centered boiler, but there the similarity ends as the cylinders drive a central gear transmiting its mechanical power to the geared wheels, which like the Shay, are actually small-diameter wheels mounted in glorified freight car trucks and powered by meshing gears. Also like the Shay, all its engine weight is on the drivers. Almost all Climaxes ever built were 2-truck types, with only a few of the 3-truck variety. The maximum weight of the very heaviest Climax was about 70-tons.

Elk River Coal and Lumber Company Climax No. 3 is shown passing through a creek using track laid in the creek bed, a common practice on logging lines, avoiding the cost of bridging. (John Krause photo, TLC Collection)

This scene, depicting Elk River's often photographed Climax No. 3 shows the locomotive at the end of a woods branch. Note the logs in the background awaiting loading. (John Krause photo, TLC Collection)

Opposite Top: This nice woodcut drawing from a Climax catalog shows the type very well, though the long wooden pilot was probably seldom if ever used in actual logging practice. (TLC Collection)

Opposite Below: In the back woods of Clay County, W. Va., Elk River Coal & Lumber Company's No. 3 Climax awaits work in the early 1950s. It is engaged in track work as evidenced by the crude cross ties on the flat car and the men behind the car working on the track. Note the long siphon hose strapped to the tender and locomotive side. The "hat" style smoke arrester caps off a tall stack. (A. A. Thieme photo, TLC Collection)

This nice Elk River Coal and Lumber scene has No. 3 with a flat car and track tools behind and a train of flats being loaded by the log loader in the left background. Another locomotive is on the log train. (John Krause photo, TLC Collection)

Spice Run Lumber Company's Climax is seen here along its logging road that connected with C&O's Greenbrier Branch at Spice Run, where the mill was located. Some type of a plate is mounted beside the straight stack, the utility of which escapes us. (TLC Collection)

Harter Lumber Company at Harter, in Pocahontas County, used this rather small Climax as its No. 1. The proportions of the locomotive and the log cars behind suggest that this may have been a narrow gauge operation. That large oil headlight really makes the locomotive look even smaller that it is. (TLC Collection)

Another view of Harter Lumber Company's No. 1 in the woods, with logs that seem to dwarf the little locomotive. (TLC Collection)

A large and powerful looking Climax No. 3 of the Moore-Kepple & Co. poses with its crew and train of big logs on the Glady & Alpina Railroad. Most Climaxes had spark arresters that were internal to the smoke box and had tall straight stacks. Look at all the gear stored on the pilot beam. This engine can now be seen on the Durbin Rocket tourist line at Durbin. (TLC Collection)

This medium sized Climax of the Tomb Lumber Company of Watoga has a conical spark arrester screen on its stack. It waits as logs are loaded on the cars in a scene from the high years of logging around 1910. (TLC Collection)

A second scene with the Tomb Lumber Company's Climax appeared in a Climax publication touting the versatility of the 42-ton machine. (TLC Collection)

Another of Spice Run Lumber's Climaxes, No. 5, has had some trouble in this scene. The good thing about small logging locomotives was that they could be righted and repaired fairly quickly by machine shops that were maintained in all the mill operations. (TLC Collection)

Snap Creek Coal Company used this small Climax to handle its coal loads from its mine across the Guyandotte River to the C&O's Logan Branch yard at Peach Creek, Logan County. This photo was made in 1948 and the little engine is about at the end of its life. A good example of a Climax in non-logging use. (Gene Huddleston Photo, TLC Collection)

This series of three photos show Climax No. 1 at work for the DeRan Lumber Company, its mill being located on the C&O Greenbrier Branch at Clover Lick.

Opposite Top: The No. 1 was Climax builder number 724, weighing 23 tons. It is on a rather impressive (for logging lines) trestle with what seems to be a rail laying train. These operations were quite common as the logging lines were shifted from one stand of timber to another. (TLC Collection)

Opposite Below: Here No. 1 is pushing a train as the logs are loaded on the right. At 23 tons the engine is on the smaller side. (TLC Collection)

Above: At the mill, No. 1 is in the distance (see the relief value exhaust) about to deliver its logs as the photographer stands on the lumber dock where men are unloading timbers from a tram. (TLC Collection)

Middle Fork Railroad Climax No. 3 at Ellamore, W. Va., in 1948. Built in 1913, the engine is nearing the end of its work on Moore Keppel Company's line. Note the coil of hose on the side of the boiler. This may have been for fire fighting. Logging locomotive crews had to be watchful of fires started by their engines. (TLC Collection)

W. H. Mason & Co. Climax No. 4 is seen here near Elkins in December 1957. It was originally Moore Keppel Middle Fork Railroad No. 4. It was eventually sold to Edaville Railroad. (TLC Collection)

Climax No. 1 "Noman" was built in 1901 and is seen here on the R. E. Woods "Tramway." This isn't a log train, but is a lumber train moving sawn lumber from the mill to the railroad connection (see next photo). Note the crude bridging! This appeared in a Climax catalog. (TLC Collection)

Also in the Climax Catalog was this drawing of Wood's No. 1. (TLC Collection)

Ely-Thomas No. 7 is seen here in for major repairs at Fenwick, with its stack capped in 1953. (Harold K. Vollrath Collection)

A couple of Climaxes used in West Virginia were not in logging service. Most prominent of these were the two or three that were owned by the shortline Cairo & Kanawha. It ran from Cairo to Grantsville, W. Va. with an addition branch 12 miles from Cairo to Mellon when chartered in 1890. By 1905 when its name became Cairo & Kanawha (former Cairo & Kanawha Valley), it was still operating 18 miles from Cairo to McFarlan. It was a 3-foot gauge line, as attested by its diminutive locomotives and equipment.

This is No. 5, one of its Climax locomotives, with a mixed passenger and freight train around 1900. Note that two of the flats have stakes as though they might be used for lumber or logs. (Mountain State Railroad & Logging Historical Association Collection)

Another view of tiny C&K No. 5, in 1928. (TLC Collection)

Here Elk River Coal and Lumber Climax No. 3 (one of the most photographed West Virginia Climaxes thanks to great railfan photographer John Krause in the 1950s) is parked next to Shay No. 19 near Swandale, W. Va., portraying the two most popular geared engines together. (John Krause photo, TLC Collection)

This very clear photo of Elk River No. 3 shows it with a work train in the summer of 1955. Note the 5-gallon can of ESSO grease on the pilot. This was a regular thing as all that gearing had to be lubricated all the time, especially since it was exposed to the elements. The tiny bobber caboose ads charm to this scene. (A. A. Thieme photo, TLC Collection)

A good overhead View of Elk River No. 3 on a track laying work train in March 1957. (John Krause photo, TLC Collection)

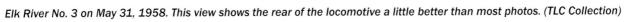

Elk River No. 3 on May 31, 1958. This view shows the rear of the locomotive a little better than most photos. (TLC Collection)

Middle Fork Railroad's Climax No. 3 is seen here out of service at Ellamore, W. Va. Middle Fork used both Climaxes and Heislers. (TLC Collection)

Elk River No. 3 rubs noses with Buffalo Creek & Gauley 2-8-0 No. 4 in BC&G's Dundon yard. The Climax, at this point (June 5, 1962) had been sold and was being tested before being shipped off to the Carroll Park & Western tourist line in New Jersey, its logging days over. (Howard W. Ameling photo)

This is entitled a "postscript" because it really is. There were only 13 Heisler locomotives that were ever bought new for use in West Virginia, so one can imagine that there are few photos. Many of those that could be located are shown in this chapter and in chapter 4 at the beginning of this book. The Heisler, though as rugged and efficient as the other two types, just never seemed to become popular in West Virginia, nor in the Appalachian forest industry region as a whole.

The Heisler required just a bit more sophistication in operation and maintenance since its driving mechanism included a gear box at the apex of the "V" shaped cylinder arrangement that was enclosed and filled with a grease bath. This was a great advantage in the respect that the gearing here was protected from the ingestion of foreign objects which was prevalent with the Shays and somewhat of a problem with the Climaxes.

The use of a driving rod on the trucks to transmit power from the single powered axle to the second axle also was apparently frowned on by the logging operators of the Appalachian region as they used few of the type.

Meadow River Lumber company's No. 6 Heisler is seen here on a snowy November day in 1959 shifting cars in the lumber company's Rainelle yard. The many C&O cabooses in the background were used on the Nicholas Fayette & Greenbrier Railroad, a joint NYC-C&O operation that tapped the Greenbrier coal fields. The line was originally built by Meadow River to gets its lumber to the C&O at Meadow Creek, but then was bought by C&O and NYC and expanded as the coal field opened up. (William E. Warden Photo, TLC Collection)

This very nice drawing from a Heisler sales catalog very clearly shows the elements and make-up of the locomotive. Characteristics are the V shaped cylinder arrangement and the connecting rod on the wheels. (TLC Collection)

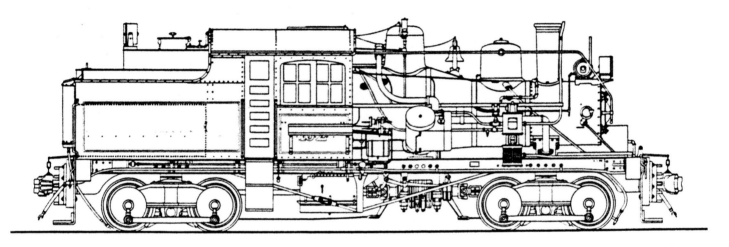

These drawings show right and left sides of two- and three-truck Heislers respectively. (TLC Collection)

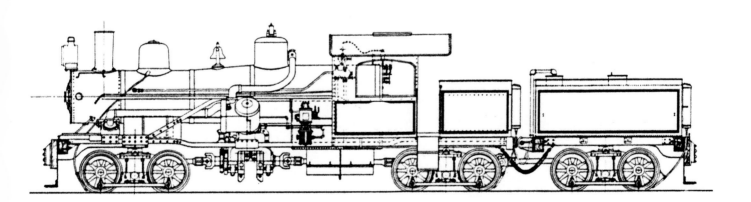

Pardee & Curtin Lumber Company of Bergoo, W. Va. got this nice looking 2-truck Heisler shown in a builder's photo. (TLC Collection)

Pardee & Curtin No. 8 here is seen in action at Bergoo in 1935 looking much more like a work-a-day locomotive even with a new diamond stack. (TLC Collection)

Meadow River Lumber Company's Heisler No. 6 is seen here with a log train in the woods near Anjean, with its ex-C&O caboose for the crew, a real luxury marking this as a high class and late era operation. Photo from about 1956. (John Krause photo, TLC Collection)

Meadow River No. 6 pauses as its heavily-built log loader loads the train from logs skidded down the slope. Meadow River ran on the NF&G (see previous captions) by trackage rights and then took to its own branches off the main line. The well-maintained NF&G line is in the background here. (John Krause photo, TLC Collection)

Meadow River Lumber Company's No. 6 was saved and is today at the Cass Scenic Railroad. This photo shows it running under its own power up the C&O's Greenbrier Subdivision toward Cass on December 15, 1968. It ran all the way from Rainelle to Cass on its own, under C&O's close supervision. (William E. Warden photo, TLC Collection)

Moore Keppel & Company's Middle Fork Railroad kept its Heisler No. 7 in operation into late days and therefore it got some railfan photographic attention. It is probably the most photographed of this rare type in West Virginia. Here No. 7 is seen from the left side at Ellamore on July 20, 1949. (TLC Collection)

Although Middle Fork's No. 7 was so well photographed, it wasn't on log trains, but on trains mainly with hopper and some box cars. Here it crosses a trestle near Cassidy with 13 loads in March 1957. (John Krause photo, TLC Collection)

The Middle Fork Heisler train is seen here amid a yard full of some kind of specialty lumber. (John Krause photo, TLC Collection)

Middle Fork had regular water tanks and looked like a normal shortline except for the usual application of Climaxes and Heislers for motive power. (John Krause photo, TLC Collection)

Another Middle Fork scene is a very clear clean scene of No. 7 with a typical Middle Fork train in the mid-1950s. (John Krause photo, TLC Collection)

Middle Fork's outlet to the world was the B&O station at Midvale, run down even at this date in the mid-1950s. (John Krause photo, TLC Collection)